Translation and Contemporary Art

This book looks to expand the definition of translation in line with Susan Bassnett and David Johnston's notion of the "outward turn", applying this perspective to contemporary art to broaden the scope of how we understand translation in today's global multisemiotic world.

The book takes as its point of departure the idea that texts are comprised of not only words but other semiotic systems and therefore expanding our notions of both language and translation can better equip us to translate stories told via non-traditional means in novel ways. While the "outward turn" has been analyzed in literature, Vidal directs this spotlight to contemporary art, a field which has already engaged in disciplinary connections with Translation Studies. The volume highlights how the unpacking of such connections between disciplines encourages engagement with contemporary social issues, around identity, power, migration, and globalization, and in turn, new ways of thinking and bringing about wider cultural change.

This innovative book will be of interest to scholars in translation studies and contemporary art.

MaCarmen África Vidal Claramonte is Full Professor of Translation at the University of Salamanca, Spain.

Translation and Contemporary Art
Transdisciplinary Encounters

**MªCarmen África
Vidal Claramonte**

Routledge
Taylor & Francis Group

NEW YORK AND LONDON

First published 2022
by Routledge
605 Third Avenue, New York, NY 10158

and by Routledge
4 Park Square, Milton Park, Abingdon, Oxon, OX14 4RN

Routledge is an imprint of the Taylor & Francis Group, an informa business

© 2022 MªCarmen África Vidal Claramonte

The right of MªCarmen África Vidal Claramonte to be identified
as author of this work has been asserted in accordance with
sections 77 and 78 of the Copyright, Designs and Patents Act 1988.

Library of Congress Cataloging-in-Publication Data
A catalog record for this book has been requested

ISBN: 978-1-032-21165-7 (hbk)
ISBN: 978-1-032-21167-1 (pbk)
ISBN: 978-1-003-26707-2 (ebk)

DOI: 10.4324/9781003267072

Typeset in Times New Roman
by Apex CoVantage, LLC

Contents

Acknowledgments

A book is always heteroglossic. It is more counterpoint than aria. Along the process of writing these pages, many melodies suggested alternative paths I had not considered, many notes sounded in my head offering different tunes. One of the most important voices was Susan Bassnett, whose ideas have had so much influence on Translation Studies over many years. Her way of understanding what translation is has been crucial to our discipline and has resulted in the definition of translation changing to adapt to our current society and becoming a discipline which is always aware of human needs. Susan Bassnett's ideas are at the starting point of this book, specifically the "outward turn" developed together with David Johnston, another outstanding translator, transgressor, and transdisciplinary for whom translating is taking words for a walk and listening to their multiple tunes. Susan Bassnett is, and for me always will be, a constant source of inspiration, not only on account of her intelligence and professionalism but also because she is one of the most thoughtful and generous people I have ever met.

I would also like to express my thanks to my colleagues and friends of the AHRC Experiential Translation Network. My membership in the experiential translation network, a group made up of artists, writers, scholars, and translators, has helped me to develop the ideas on translation I have always been passionate about. At the same time, the group has allowed me to share and compare ideas with colleagues I deeply admire, scholars like Karen Bennett and Tong King Lee, who were pioneers in research on intersemiotic translation in the fields of dance and visual arts. I would especially like to thank the constant support and inspiration of Madeleine Campbell and Ricarda Vidal who are at the head of the experiential translation network. They have been very important in the final stages of the writing of this book. I am deeply grateful to both of them for reading the text and contributing valuable ideas. No group could have better leadership.

My final thanks go to Elysse Preposi, the editor of the Routledge Focus series. Her professionalism and generosity have resulted in a trouble-free publication process.

Preface

Susan Bassnett

Translation Studies today is a well-established field, and from a relatively marginal position in the late twentieth century it has come to acquire increasing significance, notably over the last three decades, with a proliferation of books, journals, university programmes, conferences and international meetings of all kinds. Inevitably, such expansion has led to diversification, with the term 'translation studies' being interpreted differently in different contexts. Translation Studies in the twenty-first century includes the theories and practice of literary translation, the history of translation, commercial and legal translation, media translation, including dubbing and subtitling, the study of technical and machine translation and the actual training of translators and interpreters.

For the monolingual, translation is often considered to be a straightforward activity of substitution: a text created in one language is transposed into another language and the reader of the translation can be confident that nothing untoward has happened during the transfer process. But for anyone who has ever engaged with translation even at the most basic level, such a notion is absurd. Translating a text means reconfiguring it since not only do no two languages have the same alphabets, lexical items or syntax, it has long been suggested that societies live in distinct worlds, not in the same world with different labels attached and that "no two languages are ever sufficiently similar to be considered as representing the same social reality" (Sapir 1956: 69). No translation can ever be the "same" as the original, for translation involves so much more than the linguistic, though obviously language is a crucial element. As Andre Lefevere put it, translators have to deal with more than just words which may or may not have dictionary equivalents:

> Language is not the problem. Ideology and poetics are, as are cultural elements that are not immediately clear, or seen as completely

"misplaced" in what would be the target culture version of the text to be translated.

(Lefevere 1990: 26)

Lefevere made this point in an essay in the volume *Translation, History and Culture* (1990) that is generally considered to be the work that heralded the cultural turn in Translation Studies. In their preface, which was a kind of manifesto for the cultural turn, Bassnett and Lefevere argued that the object of study in the developing field had been redefined so that Translation Studies was in the process of both utilising linguistic approaches and moving out beyond them, leaving behind the old evaluative terminology of faithfulness versus betrayal and recognising that translation is a pluralistic activity, since there is always a context in which a translation takes place, a place from which a text emerges and into which that text is transposed.

If we look at what has been happening in Translation Studies since the cultural turn was first proposed thirty years ago, what can be seen is an ever-widening notion of what translation involves, indeed a widening of the very term "translation". There is a growing list of translators and translation scholars who have been instrumental in inviting us to reconsider what we understand by translation and to expand the object of study. To take just a few examples, back in 2007 Bella Brodzki argued that translation should be seen as underwriting all cultural transactions, and argued that just as gender has begun to be foregrounded in all discursive fields, so too should translation be seen as equally significant (Brodski 2007). In 2016 Piotr Blumczynski declared that translation is ubiquitous, and involves thinking about such huge questions as meaning, sense and purpose, identity, the medium and the message, the relationship between texts and individuals, about movement through space and time, about power structures and history. In 2017 Edwin Gentzler's *Translation and Rewriting in the Age of Post-Translation Studies* appeared, where he expanded on the phrase 'post-translation' coined by Siri Nergaard and Stefano Arduini in the founding issue of their journal *Translation* in 2011. For them, post-translation studies was a term that could be applied to a new era, in which translation would be viewed as transdisciplinary, mobile and open-ended. Gentzler called for an end to thinking about translation in terms of binaries (e.g., source and target) and suggested that narrow definitions of what constitutes translation were detrimental to the field. His book asks an important question:

What if translation becomes viewed less as a temporal act carried out between languages and cultures and instead as a *precondition* underlying the languages and cultures upon which communication is based?

(Gentzler 2017: 5)

Others, including Michael Cronin with his work on eco-translation, Sherry Simon and her work on the multilingual city, Lawrence Venuti with his insistence on how translation changes the way we see the world have all contributed to the broadening of ideas about translation. In his book *Contra Instrumentalism: A Translation Polemic* (2019) Venuti attacks what he sees as the instrumentalism of much traditional thinking about translation and asserts bluntly that no translation can ever provide direct or unmediated access to its source, since every text "has always already been positioned in a network of signification" (Venuti 2019: 3).

This present book is an important contribution to that broadening process and, as África Vidal puts it in her opening chapter, her work is based on the idea that today we live between boundaries, materialities, modalities, and semiotic orders. Her special concern is with contemporary art, with how to look at images and how to look through images at the world. Translation, she argues, needs now to be seen as happening through semiotic repertoires, and expanding the way we think about translation is becoming ever more urgent as we are living in a new communication landscape, one where the role of machines and electronic media in general have become so central to our lives. What we are seeing in the twenty-first century is a massive shift of perception, a movement from verbal literacy to a more multifaceted literacy, one in which the visual, aided by the digital is coming increasingly to predominate. This new multifaceted landscape presents new challenges as well as new opportunities for translation, but it is important for Translation Studies as a discipline to seize the moment.

It is also important because it is now clear that the old disciplinary boundaries created in the nineteenth and early twentieth centuries are no longer fit for purpose. Interdisciplinarity, transdisciplinarity are the new key terms, and the single subject divisions that prevailed in Western educational systems are starting to crumble. We have been witnessing new fields of research emerging such as digital Humanities, medical Humanities, Food Studies, Animal Studies, community Archaeology, Migration Studies—a whole range of fields that demand a multidisciplinary approach. Translation in all these areas has a vital role to play.

The Canadian philosopher and communication theorist Marshall McLuhan argued that human beings are shaped by the technologies they invent. He argued that the invention of a new medium can reframe our lives, as happened with the invention of paper, or the development of printing, and predicted that electronic media would bring about something he termed "the global village" (McLuhan 1962; McLuhan and Fiore 1968). He also asserted that the speed of technological changes also leads to obsolescence, as older systems that had hitherto been valued are pushed out of use. During the pandemic, when issues of global communication came to acquire a whole new significance as millions of us worked from home, cut off from regular daily exchanges with family, friends and colleagues, I went back and re-read McLuhan, and although he died before the age of the internet, his ideas do seem to have been ahead of his time. He attached great importance to temporal changes, to the accelerating speed of contemporary life, and to rapidly shifting cycles of obsolescence and retrieval. He also drew attention to the risks involved, noting how new communication technologies could become systems of control, and warning against the growth of tribalization, something that we are all aware of today with the violence and partisanship evident across social media, fueled by anonymity.

África Vidal's book develops some of the ideas in her earlier essay, 'Violins, violence, translation: looking outwards' that appeared in 2019 in a special issue of *The Translator*, titled *The Outward Turn*. She writes about the importance of the outward turn in her opening chapter of this book, stressing the need for Translation Studies to move outwards, both as a means of enriching itself and, perhaps even more importantly, as a way of increasing dialogue with other interdisciplinary fields. For although it can be argued that Translation Studies has been a success story in that it is now a globally recognised term, it is also the case that there is a risk of excessive self-referentiality and not enough has been done to share ideas about translation with researchers in other fields. Vidal sums up the current situation when she says that "we need new rules for new translation contexts if we want to understand, not only what the original text says, but *what the translation tells us"*, which means understanding its processes, views, and perceptions of the outside world. This is a book that encourages us to rethink what we understand by translation, and to reflect on the multifaceted nature of the world in which we exist and on the multiple discourses that are swirling around us, reshaping our perceptions overtly but also in deeper, less predictable ways.

References

Blumczynski, Piotr. 2016. *Ubiquitous Translation*. London and New York: Routledge.

Brodski, Bella. 2007. *Can These Bones Live? Translation, Survival and Cultural Memory*. Stanford: Stanford University Press.

Gentzler, Edwin. 2017. *Translation and Rewriting in the Age of Post-Translation Studies* London and New York: Routledge.

Lefevere, Andre. 1990. "Translation, its Genealogy in the West", in Susan Bassnett and Andre Lefevere, eds. *Translation History and Culture*. London and New York: Pinter, 14–28.

McLuhan, Marshall. 1962. *The Gutenberg Galaxy*. Toronto: University of Toronto Press.

McLuhan, Marshall, and Quentin Fiore. 1968. *War and Peace in the Global Village*. New York: Bantam.

Sapir, Edward. 1956. *Culture, Language and Personality*. Berkeley: University of California Press.

Venuti, Lawrence. 2019. *Contra Instrumentalism. A Translation Polemic*. Lincoln: University of Nebraska Press.

Vidal, África. 2019. "Violins, Violence, Translation: Looking Outwards", in Susan Bassnett and David Johnston, eds. *The Outward Turn*, special issue of *The Translator* 25, 3, September: 218–228.

1 Translating in a Visual Age: Transdisciplinary Routes

1.1 From Language to Languages: The New Texts

In *Styles of Radical Will* (1966), Susan Sontag claims that the history of art is a sequence of successful transgressions. No doubt, it is. Transgressing boundaries between disciplines allows us to observe all the worlds that fill our surroundings. These worlds are different from "our world" that sometimes alarm us with the strange differences of the "Other".[1]

We live in a global visual culture[2] where verbal language is but one component of multilingual, multimodal, and multisensory repertoires. In this context, communication implies an inevitable combination of words, images, sounds, movements, bodies, and shapes. There is no single disciplinary framework that can successfully offer an adequate approach to this multimodal world. If we want to understand how meaning is produced, expanding the idea of language helps us to attend "not only to the borders between languages but also to the borders between semiotic modes" (Pennycook 2017: 270).[3] Stories are no longer constructed with words alone but also employ a wide range of semiotic resources. Thus,

> could we not say the same of texts or writing? On this conception, a text is constituted not by language alone, but by loose clusters of features—the language (by no means a homogeneous entity), of course, but also the material-body of the text, its inscription technologies (typography, orthography, color), the affordances of the media spaces it traverses, and so forth.
>
> (Lee 2021b: 9)

This book is thus based on the idea that we live between boundaries, materialities, modalities, and semiotic orders. The transgression of boundaries between disciplines makes it possible to question solidity. Seen in this light, translation

> is no longer about moving a work from one discrete language system to another (cf. the code-view to multilingualism). It is about distributing a work through semiotic repertoires, where features from one resource cluster (encompassing and exceeding the source language) synergise with and re-embed in resources from another resource cluster, including but not limited to the target language.
>
> (Lee 2021b: 9)

Translation is now recognized "not only as an interlinguistic process but also as an intersemiotic activity across cultures and languages" (Wilson and Maher 2012: 2).

Jakobson's intersemiotic translation is hardly a new concept. It has been applied to audiovisual translation, advertising, book illustration, and other fields. However, the approach taken here is different. Our point of departure is Madeleine Campbell and Ricarda Vidal's (2019: xxix) observation that we translate "not just with the eyes but with all other senses" and Susan Bassnett and David Johnston's (2019) "outward turn in translation studies". Consequently, our aim is to analyze the connections and parallelisms between translation and contemporary art and to show how contemporary art sees and uses translation.

From this standpoint, the definition of *text* broadens considerably.[4] Many years ago, visual studies and cultural analysis expanded the interpretation of the concept of text (Bal 1985/2009). From this perspective, a text was conceived as something that was not only linguistic but which also incorporated other sign systems such as images. In her seminal work, Mieke Bal (2002) speaks of "travelling concepts" in the humanities and includes the concept of meaning and its journey between words and looks. According to Bal, the boundaries between disciplines are not dividing lines but territories in themselves or negotiation spaces. In the global era, concepts are kaleidoscopic, and they must be approached from the different disciplines that they traverse. Translating means travelling across borders (Campbell and Vidal 2019).

In today's world, images, sounds, sensory perceptions, nonverbal communication, spaces, linguistic landscapes, cities, and even bodies are considered texts because they communicate. Images have their own grammars (Kress *et al.* 1996). Visual design, oil paintings, photographs, sculptures, drawings "make meaning in different ways . . . they bring their own unique semiotic resources into play" (van Leeuwen 2021: 3). Virtual spaces and times should also be considered. "Communication happens on many levels, the gestural, the olfactory, the visual" (Campbell and Vidal 2019: xxv), apart from the linguistic (see also Finnegan 2015; Lee 2021b). Linguistic landscapes do not refer simply to language displayed in public spaces but also include images, smells, clothes, food, and graffiti. In the pandemic era, they even include masks with different kinds of messages. Applied Linguistics is also beginning to subvert traditional boundaries between language and the arts (Lee 2015b; Bradley and Harvey 2019). We attach meanings to colors (van Leeuwen 2021, 2010) and to light (Kim-Cohen 2013). Meanings are also linked to signs that look like writing but are not words. This is the case of "asemic writing", which "asks us to conceptualize what we are seeing—not reading" (Schwenger 2019: 7), for instance, Man Ray's *Poem* (1924) or Cy Twombly's *Letter of Resignation* (1967) or "black board canvases" (1970).

Sounds rewrite spaces through aural images (Blesser and Salter 2009). Sounds have political and spatial meanings that need to be interpreted and translated (Voegelin 2018; Barenboim 2008; Barenboim and Said 2003). This is also true of classical and popular music (Kaindl 2020; Mateo 2012; Hutcheon and Hutcheon in Page 2010: 65–77; McClary 1991/2002; Minors 2014; Susam-Sarajeva 2008; 2018; Vidal 2016, 2017, 2019). Noise (Serres 1982; Lingis 1994; Attali 1985/2011; Barthes 1982/1986) and silence (Serres 1983; Cage 1961, 1979; Steiner 1976) are both forms of communication, as is voice in its different forms (Barthes 1982/1986, 1986; Neumark *et al.* 2010). Contemporary hybrid and conflicted identities "manifest themselves through different uses of shape, colour, texture, timbre, and movement" (van Leeuwen 2021: 5). Even the body communicates through dance and its gestural interplay (Minors 2020; Bennett 2007, 2019; Aguiar and Queiroz 2015; Queiroz and Atã in Salmose and Elleström 2020; McCartney in Campbell and Vidal 2019: 293–309). Examples include the movement of bodies such as those in the choreographies of Matthew Bourne who translates Bizet's musical stories (Vidal 2020), or Dada Masilo's translations of *Swan Lake.*

Other examples are skinscapes, the body with its tattoos (Peck and Stroud 2015); the corporeality in physio-cybertexts of polymorphic fictions in relation to physical space, which rewrite previous stories, emotions, and feelings (Ensslin 2010). There is also the body metaphor as a semiotic system, which translates linguistic representations of the contemporary (Federici and Parlati 2018). Furthermore, contemporary art offers new ways of translating the world through painting, media art, net art, and dance (Campbell and Vidal 2019; Rizzo 2019; Mazzara 2019; Schramm *et al.* 2019; Dot 2019; Connelly 2018; Di Paola 2018a).

In the twenty-first century there is a growing recognition of discourse beyond the traditional fields. For instance, landscape and geography are understood as semiotic sites or as texts whose meanings have to be first conceptualized and then translated (Harvey 2006; Jaworski and Thurlow 2010). Museums are now regarded as translation zones (Neather in Bielsa and Kapsaskis 2021: 306–319; Sturge 2007; see also Ahrens *et al.* 2021, especially the chapter by Monika Krein-Kühle for an analysis of the translation of art discourse in the exhibition catalogue essay).

Architecture relates to language through "the semiotics of architecture," developed in Roland Barthes' 1967 lecture "Semiology and the Urban" and in Umberto Eco's "Function and Sign: The Semiotics of Architecture" (published in *The City and the Sign*. Gottdiener and Lagopoulos, eds. New York: Columbia University Press, 1986). Also interesting is the analysis of spatial texts—the study of how the built environment means—through Spatial Discourse Analysis (Ravelli and McMurtrie 2016) as well as the semiotics of movement in space, how movement may change the meaning of a particular space, the role of movement in the meaning-making process of interacting with an exhibition in a museum (the so-called "visitor studies"), buildings, and other spaces (McMurtrie 2017). Language understood as a spatial practice appears in Deleuze and Guattari's *Mille Plateaux*, in Lecercle's *The Violence of Language* and in some of Heidegger's essays (Rabourdin 2016a: 2–3). In Auster's *City of Glass* Stillman's body spells the sentence "The Tower of Babel" through the streets of New York (Rabourdin 2016b: 225–226). Architecture is therefore a discipline closely connected with language and with translation (Evans 1997). A building, Esra Akcan argues, is a text that offers cultural meanings which need to be translated (Akcan 2012, 2018). More specifically, architecture asks,

> What makes different languages interchangeable, and different places compatible with each other? How do products and ideas pertaining to visual culture, art, and architecture get translated, and what are the ethical and political consequences of these translations? . . . Is the ethical translation the one that resists the implementation of a new set of standards in the local context and appropriates the imported artifact into the local conditions, or the one that refuses to assimilate the foreign into the local and intentionally manifests the foreignness of the translated artifact? Who speaks and who cannot speak during the process of translation?
>
> (Akcan 2012: 6)

In this venue, cities have become new translated/translating texts (Lee 2013a, 2021a; Simon 2012, 2019; Pennycook and Otsuji 2015).[5] Moving through these spaces, "[w]e construct meaning by the incremental experience we have of words" (Rabourdin 2016b: 230). The relationship between "linguistic translation and spatial translation . . . offers a complex and fertile relationship" (Rabourdin 2020: 3). "Writing" (and I would add, translating) "involves the whole body" (Rabourdin 2020: 3). Translating across borders creates new connections between cultures and media "by perceiving and experiencing non-verbal media through visual, auditory and other sensory channels" (Campbell and Vidal 2019: xxvi).

Signs are transposed into different semiotic forms (Pârlog 2019). Our contemporary semiotic landscape is more complex than ever because we communicate within a context where globalization has boosted technological development. Literacy has moved into the digital age and transformed the humanities in the postprint era (Hayles and Pressman 2013) of non-physical spaces (Mitchell 2003). Since the expansion of television in the 1970s and video in the 1980s, cultural habits have shifted from books to audiovisual media. Evidently, books no longer occupy the cultural place they once held, now that reading media have diversified from paper to digital. The texts/images with which we read the world today appear in places that were previously unthinkable, such as Facebook, Google, blogs, You-Tube, Twitter, or Instagram.

Many new modes and genres are used as new ways to tell stories where words are no longer so prominent as they once were. Graphics and animation have transformed the visual richness of these texts into a challenge for translators. These new texts have altered the traditional conceptions of plot, structure, temporality, originality, and agency. At the same time they are vivid proof that words are only one of many semiotic systems which may be used to communicate (Jewitt 2009: 14; Page 2010: 3–10; Page and Thomas 2011: 1–4).

Communication today includes the new textual condition and digital metroliteracies (Dovchin and Pennycook 2017). In these new contexts, it is necessary to envisage the full range of communication forms used and their interrelationships, which appear in Web-based homepages, digital fiction, born digital hypertexts narratives, gaming, hyperlinked words, electronic literature, the photo-sharing application Flickr, and YouTube. There are also sites that use WordPress where individuals narrate their stories on blogs, journals, and discussion boards, or Facebook, with its collaborative story-telling ventures, wall posts, comments, and microblogging.

In the era of multimodality, in which

> semiotic modes other than language are treated as fully capable of serving for representation and communication . . . language, whether as speech or as writing, may now often be seen as ancillary to other semiotic modes: to the visual for instance. Language may now be "extra

visual". The very facts of the new communicational landscape have made that inescapably the issue.

(Kress and van Leeuwen 2001: 46)

This panorama has given way to a constant translation of the verbal into the visual and vice versa (Clarke 2007), to a visual representation of information, to new audiovisual messages—in short, to the transition from monomodal to multimodal texts (Kress 2003, 2010; Kress and van Leeuwen 2001).[6]

Given this situation, new scholarship about language, cognition, and communication opens new venues for research (Pennycook 2018) in translation. Translators need a nonlinear, complex, interactive way of thinking (Morin 1990/2008; Marais and Meylaerts 2019), beyond binarisms. Translation is a tangible, daily, necessary, and indispensable experience of contemporary life. "I link, therefore I am" (Mitchell 2003: 62), says the nodular subject. In such a changing, interwoven, mobile, cosmopolitan, and liquid society, translation has ceased to be merely interlinguistic, because the new surroundings in which it takes place force the translator to continually cross spaces and forge new *topoi* from familiar *loci*.

In short, communication and translation appear today in contexts which go beyond traditional languages (Marais 2019). Communication studies, sociolinguists and others include new terms, such as intermediality, intermodality, multimediality, and multimodality, transposition, transmediation, transmodality, translanguaging, transmedia navigation, transcreation, adaptation, semiotranslation, interart, voice description, respiratory narrative, body metaphor, cinematization, gamification, metafilmic, kinekphrastic, transideology, interfigurality, and so on (Elleström 2010, 2019, 2021; Salmose and Elleström 2020; Clüver 2007, 2019; Ensslin 2010; García and Li 2014; Lee and Li 2020; Federici and Parlati 2018). Hence, communication "is not just about going *between* languages. It is also about going *within*, where the intralingual and interdiscursive dimensions of text and talk complement the interlingual, as well as going *beyond* (language as such), hence beyond the code-view of multilingualism, encompassing various other material and sensory modalities" (Lee 2021b: 6. See also Kress and van Leeuwen 2001 and Jan Bloomaert's publications for the social semiotics view of language and other modalities as mobile semiotic resources).

The very facts of this new communication landscape have made the question of exploring the limits of language and representation an important issue. It is necessary to acknowledge the power of the invisible, and to discover ways to grasp the possibilities of the new texts which include "the real unseen that opens and gestures towards the idea of alternatives" (Voegelin 2018: 5). This does not mean avoiding the politics of everyday life but finding innovative pathways to access the new ways we communicate via sounds, bodies, gestures, images, colors, and forms. In other words, this book is about a new and enlarged definition of translation or translation as a successful transgression of boundaries between disciplines, to say it with Susan Sontag (1966). In this sense, translation is a transdiscipline that keeps us moving by creating tensions and dialogues that explore those fragments of creative productions which trigger our curiosity. It offers new responses "to the failings of a complete and reasonable world" (Voegelin 2018: 5–7).

1.2 Expanding Translation

As previously suggested, in our global and cosmopolitan world the possible range of codes and sign systems has multiplied. This diversity highlights the need to consider the new forms of communication that have emerged. In the transnational society, translation moves along borders, in multilingual spaces, in post-colonial hybrid environments where languages struggle to overcome asymmetry within cosmopolitanism (Bielsa 2016a). The globalization of markets, but also the globalization of fear, violence, and poverty in a liquid society (Bauman 2000, 2006, 2007, 2016), have made it impossible to ignore translation. As a result, in these new multimodal contexts, Translation Studies moves beyond strict textual analysis to broader research paradigms. The new texts (including videogames, Web sites, song covers, illustrations, icons, tweets, films, graphic novels, dance performances, songs, and many others) demand new composite and heterotypical translation processes across various media.

Expanding the field of Translation Studies is thus an urgent goal, since the stories told through non-traditional modes need to be translated in novel ways. Within this new semiotic landscape, translation must broaden its scope. It is beginning to expand beyond the verbal (Pérez-González 2014). Developments in multimodal studies (Boria *et al.* 2020) have already begun to change our idea of what translation is. In fact, many scholars claim that in our global culture "the question of what constitutes a translation is under radical review" (Gentzler 2015: 2; see also Bassnett and Johnston 2019). The task of the translator is no longer between two languages but rather between

> many contemporary parts of social life. . . . From this perspective, it is possible to view all language use as a process of translation, thus questioning the assumption that translation is a mapping of items from one code to another . . . all communication involves translation.
>
> (Otsuji and Pennycook in Lee 2021a: 59)

In this context, translation is ubiquitous. It means reflecting

> on much larger issues, such as meaning, sense, and purpose; identity, sameness and similarity; the relationship between part and whole; between the message and its medium; between ideas; between texts; between individuals; between individuals and texts; between communities; between texts and communities; between different times and places; between what is fixed and what is dynamic; between exercising force and experiencing influence, and so on. Translation takes us into a surprisingly broad range of territories and confronts us with the most fundamental of questions . . . to me, translation is—at least potentially—everywhere.
>
> (Blumczynski 2016: ix, xiii)

As Blumczynski argues, when we translate translation into other areas, translating creates a surplus of meaning by opening horizons of possibilities. It offers "a different way of facing the great epistemological questions of what we know and how we know" (Arduini and Nergaard 2011: 9). From this perspective, sense can only be met in our complex and diverse world through "interdisciplinary connections" (Gentzler 2003), through a methodology *sans borders* which blurs its boundaries in order to find new openings for translation (Brems *et al*. 2014: 2).

Translation is a way to displace institutionalized forms of recognition with thinking:

> To *think* (rather than to seek to explain) in this sense is to invent and apply conceptual frames and create juxtapositions that disrupt and/or render historically contingent accepted practices. It is to compose the discourse of investigation with critical juxtapositions that unbind what are ordinarily presumed to belong together and thereby to challenge institutionalized ways of reproducing and understanding phenomena.
>
> (Shapiro 2013: xv)

The assumption is that the translator's task is to *think* in Shapiro's sense, to create juxtapositions beyond media borders (Elleström 2021) in dynamic contexts which exist between and across boundaries, and also beyond monolingual spaces and exclusionary practices. The contemporary translator's repertoire is composed of "different semiotic orders" (Baynham and Lee 2019a: 18), and within the new spaces, s/he needs to move from language to consider the materiality and affordances of "the visual, the gestural, and what can be communicated with the body or, to be more precise, by the body" (Baynham and Lee 2019a: 97). This involves translanguaging into the intersemiotic, multimodal domain, which obliges translators to use a spectrum of semiotic resources to extend their repertoire.

Translating today is a heterotopic activity that exists between different spaces and epistemological times. It is an activity that crosses, not only all contemporary arts, from music, painting, and dance to literature, but also every moment of our life, from birth to death. This book proposes that the same concept is present in different epistemological areas and thus leads to decentred, aterritorial translation. This is translation as a series "of created relatedness, between embodied selves, interacting with different cognitive, affective and sensorial environments, and other equally embodied selves for whom those environments are, to a greater or lesser extent, other" (Johnston 2013: 369).

Within this context, translation becomes a way of exploring our relationship with language(s) through its physical and sensory effects on our bodies. Translation allows us to access meaning as *becoming*, in the sense of Deleuze and Guattari in *A Thousand Plateaux* and in the *Anti-Oedipe*. From this perspective, *becoming* is the point at which two different entities connect by means of a network of infinite relationships. This is why the *becoming* is a frontier phenomenon, an experience of/between the limit of both physical and emotional spaces. According to Edwin Gentzler (2015: 2),

> rather than thinking about translation as a somewhat secondary process of ferrying ideas across borders, we think beyond borders to culture as a whole, reconceiving translation as an always primary, primordial, and proactive process that continually introduces new ideas, forms or expressions, and pathways for change into cultures: translation without borders.

By taking visual literature, dance, painting, and music as new territories where translation is defined, we set off on a journey through disciplines which do not contradict each other but improve on one another by crossing thresholds. Thus, in these new texts, translating is a concept that not only travels between the lines, from words to paintings as in ekphrasis,[7] but also between sounds, colors, or dancing bodies. With this transversality of disciplines, "each of us is a bundle of fragments of other people's souls, simply put together in a new way" (Hofstadter 2007: 252), that we are strange loops where everything is interrelated, and this gives us "a deeper and subtler vision of what it is to be human" (*ibid.*: 361).

Our contemporary world does not only translate with words because, as Douglas R. Hofstadter (1997: 44) points out in *Gödel, Escher, Bach*, "it is all about translation". The concepts of similarity, paradox, self-representation, identity, and meaning are always present on this journey and will take us into the unknowns of the different semiotic systems when we reach the limits of self-reference. In fact, this is what happens when two mirrors facing each other are forced to reflect each other indefinitely (Hofstadter 1979/2013: 182–185).

Hofstadter analyzes all these concepts in Gödel's mathematical logic, in Escher's drawings, and in Bach's music. He demonstrates that the three addressed the same notions in fields apparently far removed from each other. His work highlights the fact that they express continuity in the discontinuous as well as alternation and simultaneity with the discontinuous in the continuous. In this respect, Gödel's incompleteness theorem stems from the same principle as Escher's "picture within the picture". For example, with its concave or convex architectural spaces, the question is whether his characters are going up or down. The theorem is also based on the Epimenides paradox or the Moebius strip, that unorientable loop.

Especially impressive is Hofstadter's analysis of the palindrome which is Bach's so-called "Crab Canon", and how it relates to Escher's "Crab Canon" and to Gödel's Typographical Number Theory (TNT), all based on the concept of self-reference (Hofstadter 1979/2013: 222ff). In this sense, the most outstanding example of Bach's counterpoint is found in the final "Contrapunctus" of *The Art of Fugue*, the last fugue he composed, where his name is hidden in the last part (using the "translation" of letters into notes: B flat, A, C H natural). Not surprisingly Bach, occasionally, also created acrostics. In fact, the B-A-C-H melody if played backwards is exactly the same as the original (Hofstadter 1979/2013).

Also intriguing is the relationship that he establishes between Bach's wonderful "Canon per Tonos", from *The Musical Offering*, and Escher's *Waterfall* (1961) or *Up and Down* (1947). As Hofstadter says in a much later work, music is

> a direct route to the heart or between hearts—in fact, the most direct. Across-the-board alignment of musical tastes, including loves and hates [—] is a sure guide to affinity of souls as I have ever found. And an affinity of souls means that the people concerned can rapidly come to know each other's essences, have great potential to love inside each other.
>
> (Hofstadter 2007: 250)

Composing is a desperately difficult task, says the Devil in *Doktor Faustus*. The same is true of creation through painting, music, the body, and words. In all these cases, the work only reveals its meanings when we interpret it, or when we use it to express our passions, fears, and desires, in the limbo between the creature born from the solitude of the artist and our own self. Against the monotony of the verb *be*, the translator is a Heideggerian *being* in the world. In the face of permanence, constant flux, movement, unlimited transferal of words, images, or music allows us to see to what extent translation is the phenomenon at the root of all these practices.

This new "Translation Zone(s)", as proposed by Heather Connelly (2018) explore the nature of translation between disciplines which are always "intranslation". She is referring to disciplines that belong "to no single, discrete language or single medium of communication" (Apter 2006: 6). This is a zone cast by artists, musicians, dancers, painters, photographers, and translators, which extracts us from the comfort zone of monolingualism and transforms translation into a medium of political and social change. Connelly's "Translation Zone(s)" is a polyvocal project where she

> researches the non-linguistic aspects of translating and vocalising a foreign language's basic phonic constituents, thereby challenging the semiotic representation of sign systems to achieve new and enhanced aesthetic and cultural understanding. In a step-by-step account of her intersemiotic translation process, she eschews the symbolic aspects of a language's written alphabet or script, to embrace its sensory and affective dimensions.
>
> (Campbell and Vidal 2019: xxxv, 217–246)

As is well known, the initial prescriptivist vision of translation which defended absolute equivalence and neutrality was rejected because of a widespread dissatisfaction with traditionalist views of translation as an objectivized empirical enterprise in which the translator is impartial and invisible. This vision of translation gradually changed, thanks to a number of factors such as the following: (i) the polysystem theorists of the 1960s; (ii) books such as *Translation Studies* published by Susan Bassnett in 1980; (iii) the concept of manipulation resulting from Theo Hermans's seminal anthology published in 1985; (iv) Mary Snell-Hornby's interdisciplinary turn in 1988; and (v) the cultural turn introduced by Bassnett and Lefevere in their influential "Proust's Grandmother and the Thousand and One Nights" (1990). This was followed by André Lefevere's *Translation, Rewriting, and the Manipulation of Literary Fame* (1992), which applied Michel Foucault's concept of power to translation, and was the first exploration of power relations within textual practice. In 2002 in another seminal anthology, Maria Tymoczko and Edwin Gentzler established what they called "the power turn in Translation Studies", which eventually led to the development of postcolonial translation studies and feminist translation theories.

All of this meant that translating was no longer understood as a pure, neutral activity, in the same way that writing is never innocent. The translator thus became an increasingly visible agent within the translation process rather than a faithful servant. The "sociological turn" (Wolf and Fukari 2007) is closely connected with the cultural turn (Zwischenberger 2019). The next "turn", the so-called "translational turn" (Bachmann-Medick 2009), reveals the expansion and relevance of the processes of cultural translation in multicultural societies. Building on Bhabha's conception of cultural translation, the proponents of the translational turn use the concept in two ways. The first way is to convey ideas, values, behaviors, and patterns of thought, and the second is to denote inter- or transdisciplinary translation. In this second sense, it is closely connected to Mieke Bal's "travelling concepts" (Bachmann-Medick 2016a: 119–136; Blumczynski 2016). Subsequently, the "technological turn" (Cronin 2010) appeared, followed by "post-translation" (Gentzler 2017) and the "outward turn" (Bassnett and Johnston 2019).

Certainly, the changes in our discipline, especially since the 1980s, have been spectacular. The incorporation of concepts such as manipulation, ideology, power, asymmetry, representation, and so on, initially seemed to indicate that Translation Studies could become a subversive field, attentive to the power games between the cultures of our global world. However, for some years now, perhaps because of the institutionalization of the discipline, Translation Studies have focused on being recognized as an independent degree in the university curriculum. After the successive turns, there is now danger that it will be embedded in the universities as part of the syllabus and become a "self-contained discipline with its own models and paradigms". This could result in a kind of isolation that can only become complacency, in a discipline that is "marketable", "chic", and "sexy", "the term of the moment" (Bassnett 2011: 72):

> Perhaps we have concentrated too hard on becoming respectable, on claiming to be a discipline, that we have lost our cutting edge. Nothing leads to complacency faster than success; the time has come for those of us who would like to think of ourselves as translation studies scholars to rethink not only how we have come to be here, but where and with whom we want to go next.
>
> (Bassnett 2014a: 25)

In this venue, Cornelia Zwischenberger ensures that translation may be considered as a prototype of Bal's previously mentioned "travelling concept", as it has travelled to numerous disciplines in recent years. Even though she also points out that "translation" is used

> as a very broad metaphor in neighbouring disciplines and fields of research of Translation Studies, this mobility also reveals the potential and high polysemantic value of the translation concept. What is missing, however, is a "translaboration" between translation studies and the various other disciplines that employ translation studies' master concept.
>
> (Zwischenberger 2017: 388)

She goes on to say that, although ethnography, anthropology, or sociology, among many other disciplines, have already adopted the concept of translation in a broad sense—something that Bachmann-Medick (2009, 2012) pointed out a few years ago—our discipline has not yet been able to make the leap into other territories (Zwischenberger 2017). In contrast, both in art and in many other disciplines, translation has been used, often without explicitly naming it: " it is rather us, both as translators and translation researchers, who travel through these disciplines—only to discover that certain kinds of translational thought and practice are somehow already present in the territories we visit" (Blumczynski 2016: 2).

Indeed, there are still many types of translation that have not gone as far as the art world has. Perhaps the most obvious sign that much remains to be done is that in many non-specialized contexts, the translator is still a mere transmitter of meanings and is expected to be invisible. Something similar happens for example in the case of certain foreign language teachers who use translation to show their students that the meaning of the original text is closed and that a single univocal translation can be made of it. What is even worse is when this occurs in institutional and legal contexts, where it is especially dangerous to persist in the idea that the translator or interpreter can achieve absolute equivalence. When institutions expect interpreters to transmit the "truth" in a neutral way, the failure to take into account the social, cultural, or political issues of each situation or the differences between the different judicial systems is, at the very least, problematic. Fortunately, there are now many excellent studies that have incorporated concepts from other disciplines into legal and institutional translation (see Martín Ruano 2018).

For this reason, Yves Gambier (2016: 887) states that "translation has more often than not seemed to serve the powers that be, ostensibly beholden to established authorities" and that "many sponsors, amateurs, self-translators (including scholars translating their own articles), and engineers within the language industry continue to consider translation as a mechanical process, a word-by-word substitution, a problem of dictionaries, or simply an activity that accrues no apparent prestige and which can be handed off at any moment to a bilingual relative or colleague." And if we add the complacency, the "inward turn" of Translation Studies as a discipline, it seems urgent at this point to rethink translation processes and begin to actively discuss the conditions for an "outward turn in translation studies", or "a greater openness towards interdisciplinarity", as understood by Brems *et al.* (2014: 5). Furthermore, this necessary "interdisciplinary turn" of translation studies referred to by Gentzler (2003: 22) must lead to a "translational turn" in other areas.

What Bassnett and other authors fear is that there has been a step backwards, and that instead of looking outward, Translation Studies has begun to look inward, prioritizing its own curricula, high-impact journals, publishers, and series whose focus is on translation, international conferences, and increasingly institutionalized meetings. Although the pioneers of this shift toward more revolutionary definitions of translation initially were the key to great progress, they realized just in time that, given the current state of the art, we cannot afford to inhabit an isolated conceptual space but rather just the opposite. Translation Studies, which is now recognized as a discipline, must emerge and embrace other areas of knowledge and research methodologies in order to become a truly interdisciplinary field. This is a basic and necessary characteristic in a hybrid, complex, mestizo world such as ours.

From this new starting point, the constant indefinition of translation is promising. The new definition of translation—" 'indefinition' should be functional and emergent (in a constant state of Deleuzean becoming), rather than static, more about what it does than what it is", as Madeleine Campbell argues (personal communication). It should also aim to overcome the dangerous and impoverishing Eurocentrism that was beginning to characterize our field (Dollerup 2008; Tymoczko 2007; van Doorslaer and Flynn 2013). The next step should be to draft a new map of power relations and multicultural dialogues in an increasingly wide range of domains, from the legal and scientific to literature and the arts. The status of translation as an independent discipline should not come at the cost of a dangerous isolationism (Brems *et al.* 2014: 9–10). An interdisciplinary perspective will allow us to better analyze those multilingual and multidisciplinary spaces (Simon 2019, 2012; Lee 2021a; Vidal 2012) which the global world has become.

The methodology, point of view, and the very definition of translation is thus what must begin to change (Hermans 2002; Gentzler 2003). This is the best way to move toward other epistemological fields, beyond traditionally established boundaries, undermining the paradigms previously accepted as valid. Consequently, translation will focus "on broader translinguistic aspects and transcultural processes" (Bassnett 2011: 72) to become an open and dynamic discipline, a field of research in constant movement, capable of covering "an impressive spectrum of topics approachable by means of a no less impressive set of tools or methods" (D'hulst and Gambier 2018: 1). These tools and methods, which are no doubt shared with other disciplines, will give our field an intellectual dynamism and an interdisciplinarity with plural, kaleidoscopic visions, very consistent with the hybrid cosmopolitan world of our activity. Movement and travelling concepts are the unstable foundation on which the new way of understanding translation will be established because movement is related to the questions that we ask and how we ask them. The journey creates new landscapes, as well as innovative and enriching ideas. If we want to think critically, we need to move, because static thinking is usually a covert form of control. Movement precedes thought, according to a Tibetan saying:

> when movement initiates and opens thinking we are not only courting the possible advent of the unknown . . . but we are also putting ourselves in a humble or learning relationship to the knowledge and experiences of others. We bring, we test, we transmit, but we also change and allow ourselves to be changed.
>
> (Breytenbach 2009: 6)

Translation is the ideal space for these interactions in movement with other cultures, "[a]nd when one says *movement* one is talking rhythms and patterns, contrasts and contradictions and contestations, maybe conflict, hybridism and survival consciousness, the intensified interaction between the known and the unknown" (Breytenbach 2009: 6).

Translation Studies is becoming aware of the need to build new transdisciplinary research methodologies that will help us to solve the challenges presented by texts created with images, sounds, or bodies. Such texts provide as much or more meaning than texts solely composed of words. However, their translation is infinitely more complex, because it is necessary to take into account what is and what is not an image, the perspective from which the text has emerged, the colors used and what those colors and bodies mean in different cultures. In a constantly changing world, "translating has become a notion to be negotiated instead of being a ready-made concept" (Brems *et al.* 2014: 11). This is precisely what Translation Studies is becoming. Transcending Roman Jakobson's structuralist framework, Translation Studies highlights the need to be aware of surroundings as well as the context of social and technological change in which the translator currently works. It reflects the fact that translation is no longer only a written task, but now involves painting, dancing, listening, watching: "not just source to target, but to target and beyond, west to east, north to south, linear to non-linear, text to images, and forward in time and space through multiple languages, cultures and genres" (Gentzler 2017: 112–113).

Translation unveils the world around us and is able to make important contributions to those surroundings that inevitably surprise us, both positively and negatively, every day. Broadening the limits of translation is an urgency that many theorists have long argued for (Hermans 2001; Gentzler 2003; Tymoczko 2007; Gambier 2006, 2014; Gambier and van Doorslaer 2009; Bassnett 2011; Johnston 2017; Marais 2019). Of course, they are aware that this involves incorporating new concepts, disciplines, and challenges (Delabastita 2003). The only way forward is to "wander around different areas . . . change the way of thinking by asking unusual questions or that [we find] in foreign territories" (García Canclini 2014: 31).

Many publications and conferences[8] are beginning to move in this direction (Dam *et al.* 2019; Campbell and Vidal 2019; Ott and Weber 2019; Gambier and van Doorslaer 2016; Brems *et al.* 2014). There are also interesting initiatives, such as that of Madeleine Campbell on intersemiotic translation[9] or the so-called "translaboration" of Alexa Alfer and Cornelia Zwischenberger, which has led to various publications (Alfer 2015, 2017; Zwischenberger 2017, 2019) as well as a monographic issue of *Target* (2020). These new ways of understanding translation are broadening its definition by considering that a text is not only created with words but also with multiple semiotic systems. This is reflected in the monographic issues of Translation Studies journals (*JoSTrans* 35 January 2021, *The Translator* 25, 3, 2019, *Target* 2020, *Punctum* 6, 1, 2020, *Translation Matters* 1, 2, 2019, *Art in Translation* 10, 1, 2018) that specifically focus on this topic. Translation has become multilayered, heterotopical and heterotypical, and is

> understood as practices of adaptation that amalgamate cultures and transform meaning. In this sense, translation does not simply occur between two languages or cultural spheres. Instead, it is shaped by a continuous process of cultural and media transformation that takes place between different semiotic registers.
>
> (Ott and Weber 2019: 7)

Some decades ago, scholars like Peeter Torop[10] (1995) applied the concept of translation to any type of cultural communication. Culture was defined as an infinite process of *total* translation, where texts composed of one substance, for example, the verbal, are translated to other semiotic systems. Gambier and van Doorslaer (2016) propose "border crossing" by charting the intersections of translation with other academic fields such as biosemiotics, cognitive neuroscience, sociology, gender studies, and military history. Scholars such as Piotr Blumczynski (2016) examine the role of translation in fields like anthropology, philosophy, and theology, whereas others question the semantic effect of images and multimodality on an increasingly transnational, multisemiotic, and multimodal communicative landscape (Oittinen *et al.* 2019; Olteanu *et al.* 2019; Weissbrod and Kohn 2019; Dicerto 2018; Desjardins 2017; Gardner and Martín Ruano 2015; Kaindl 2013; Gardner 2010).

The multimodal approach to communication is also generating a considerable number of publications in Translation Studies to respond to the challenges of the new texts.[11] Translation, traditionally centered on the verbal, needs to develop "appropriate investigation instruments for non-language modes" (Kaindl 2013: 266. See also Lee 2021b; Pérez-González 2014; Adami 2016; Ramos Pinto and Adami 2020; Dicerto 2018; O'Sullivan and Jeffcote 2013; Jiménez Hurtado *et al.* 2018), since meaning "is a multifaceted, context-dependent and mutable phenomenon which inevitably dissipates and alters during the translation process, losing some layers and gaining others, and occasionally transmuting into something altogether different" (Bennett 2019: 1).

Some scholars understand intersemiotic translation as adaptation (Giannakopoulou 2019; Raw 2012) whereas others describe translation as a valuable art form (Malmkjær 2019) or as transcreation (Katan 2016; Spinzi *et al.* 2018). All these approaches, together with new modes of translations, such as transduction, recreation, intericonicity, multimodal and intermedial translation, fansubbing (Massidda 2015), crowdsourcing (Jiménez Crespo 2017), and collaborative translation (Cordingley and Manning 2017), challenge the traditional structure of the translation market, or the agency and ethics of the discipline. They problematize translation (Marais 2019) and encourage new research in Translation Studies (Spinzi *et al.* 2018). In line with this book, some clearly associate translation with the ways of looking at the world from/with contemporary art in all its forms, namely, painting, photography, dance, music, films, media art, and so on (Boria *et al.* 2020; Campbell and Vidal 2019; Ott and Weber 2019; Dot 2019; Di Paola 2015, 2018a, 2018b; Vidal 2017, 2019; Rizzo 2019). Translation is a multidirectional activity that

> necessarily shifts the focus toward artistic productions, as they frequently constitute cultural and media composites . . . an interplay between not just different languages and their modal forms of expression but also between different media articulations, between image, tone, and sound, between material installation, a given spatial ambience, and patterns of reception, and between configurations of protagonists and viewers.
>
> (Ott and Weber 2019: 8)

All these scholars and many others warn against univocal definitions of translation and urge us to bear in mind the new surroundings that translators explore in search of future lines of research. Now is the time to look back in order to move forward. This means starting from the first of the turns, the cultural turn, which contributed so much to understanding new ways of translation, and going all the way to the technological turn. It also involves a reflection on how the contemporary world has changed, which points to the need to reexamine "conventional understandings of what constitutes translation and the position of the translator" (Cronin 2010: 1), and from there to the most contemporary turn, the "outward turn".

In what follows, I will focus on the latest turn in Translation Studies, the outward turn, as a methodology to expand the definition of translation by taking it into an area in constant movement between the blurred limits of a discipline in continuous approximation to others. This is also a way of further enriching those spaces, which are more and more *sans borders* (Gentzler 2015), where translation has settled. Since this will no doubt generate new ethical questions (Spinzi *et al.* 2018; Baker 2014: 21ff; see also Folaron in D'hulst and Gambier 2018: 127–133), the translator's response will also have to be new. As observed by Delabastita (2003: 9), "Translation Studies had to be invented, apparently, to show how blurred and how elusive a concept translation really is".

1.3 Toward the "Outward Turn"

The origin of the "outward turn", this new way of understanding translation as an activity open to other disciplines, was an article by Stefano Arduini and Siri Nergaard, "Translation: A New Paradigm" (2011), published in *Translation: a Transdisciplinary Journal*. The subtitle of this journal clearly expresses the new conception of translation that encourages transdisciplinarity as a way of going "beyond the traditional borders of the discipline", and opening up to art, architecture, ethnography, studies on memory, psychology, philosophy, and economics. It is also revealing to look at the term "transdisciplinarity". Compared to "interdisciplinarity", which is based on the "what", *trans* is based on the "how", a how that invites paradox, tensions, discontinuity, and which recognizes deconstruction and the dissemination of limits.

Interdisciplinary is arboreal, whereas transdisciplinary is rhizomatic in the Deleuze and Guattari sense.[12] It is in this way that Arduini and Nergaard (2011: 9) understand translation. In other words, transdisciplinary research "cannot follow linear paths that conceive of structures as trees, but must rather walk along rhizomatic paths". For these authors, the need to redefine translation is not negative but quite the opposite.

While some express concern about an ill-defined and delimited concept, we are of the view that such an approach is a strength and that any premature and a priori definition of the limits and borders of translation prevents us from evolving new theories and changing our assumptions and directions.

(2011: 12)

The "outward turn" (Bassnett and Johnston 2019; Bassnett 2011, 2014a, 2014b, 2016; Johnston 2013, 2017) emerges in this context. The aim of this turn is to see translation "taught in programmes across the board, integrated into studies of all kinds, including Medicine, Law, Business, the sciences, and not just within the Humanities or as an add-on to foreign language learning" (Bassnett 2017b: 146). Bassnett shares a concern about the state of Translation Studies as a field, about its inability to move forward and its failure to have much impact on other disciplines. In her view,

we have missed an opportunity to form an intellectual group that would be concerned with promoting translation as a creative act, one which always involves language and is also political, but which above all is a process of discovery. We learn through translating—we learn about our own language as well as about the language from which we are translating. We learn what cannot be said, what is unsayable, and we also learn about compromise, manipulation, negotiation. I go so far as to believe that it ought to be possible—indeed essential—to teach translation to people who have no foreign language, because in a way everyone engages in intralingual and intersemiotic translation, to go back to good old Jakobson, even if they don't have a foreign language. I think this is what Gentzler is trying to say through his post-translation studies stuff.

(Bassnett 2017b: 150)

What Bassnett means by "outward" is a combination involving two directions of outwardness:

firstly, Translation Studies needs to reflect on why so much of Translation Studies thinking has not made its way into other disciplines and also why so much innovative thinking is coming from world literature and comparative literature not Translation Studies; and secondly, Translation Studies needs to engage more with other disciplines rather than, as we fear has been happening, with Translation Studies becoming introspective and scholars only talking to one another.

(personal communication)

The outward turn is necessary because even though there are already indicators of change as reflected in relevant publications, "translation studies practitioners have not managed to reach out sufficiently to other fields and all too often talk only to one another" (Bassnett in Gentzler 2017: ix). Translating outwards calls for the expansion of the discipline's self-imposed boundaries. It shows that "all translation is a vivid demonstration of interdependency" (Cronin 2003: 3). The new turn broadens the limits of the discipline to the point of understanding that image, music, cinema, sculpture, painting, dance, and architecture are, as previously mentioned, texts in movement that involve "visual translations" (Akcan 2012: 7). Such texts are transformations of meaning with non-linguistic elements which are ultimately translations of the Real:

> Definitions of language are changing, challenged by proliferating semiotic codes and sign systems, informed by new technologies for the construction of texts, and complicated by factors associated with dialects and emerging languages. Definitions of what constitutes a text are also changing, as more oral and performative texts are included in studies. Lines between translation, adaptation, abridgement, paraphrase, and summaries are blurring.
>
> (Gentzler 2013: 11)

The outward turn may be a useful way to approach translation in the era of multiplicity of semiotic systems since they allow us to widen horizons to a changing, mobile definition of our task (Gentzler 2014: 23):

> Translation scholars need to look beyond the linguistic and literary to music, lights, set, costumes, gestures, make-up, and facial expressions to better understand this new intercultural and intersemiotic age of translation. As the media changes, so too do the performance options increase, and more dynamic theories of translation and internationalization are needed for the future.
>
> (Gentzler 2017: 217)

Translation is today a phenomenon that appears in all languages through very different forms of communication, not only in written texts. Translation is now present in all areas:

> *every* discipline derives from and depends upon translation, a dependency that will only increase in the future. Contemporary and increasingly interdisciplinary studies of translation suggest that the borders transgressed in translation tend to be more multiple and permeable than traditionally conceived. . . . What if translation becomes viewed less as a temporal act carried out between languages and cultures and instead

as a *precondition* underlying the language and cultures upon which communication is based? What if we consider the political, social, and economic structures as built upon translation? What if we view the landscape—the parks, buildings, roads, memorials, churches, schools, and government organizations—not as solely monocultural, but also as a product of post-translation effects?

(Gentzler 2017: 5)

Gentzler puts his ideas into practice by analyzing the post-translations that have been made of Shakespeare, Goethe, or Proust. This book will show that it is indeed possible to erase the boundaries between disciplines and take the concept of translation to the extreme by analyzing contemporary works of art as artistic forms that communicate, as semiotic systems that transmit information through interwoven channels. One example is Sherrie Levine, a photographer who "copies", post-translates, Walker Evans or Joan Miró without any attempt to disguise it in a way reminiscent of Yedda Morrison's translation of the 1997 Kyoto Protocol on climate change. This type of graphic text might be compared with Marcel Broodthaers's edition of/rewriting of Stéphane Mallarmé's *A coup de dés*, "which replaced the poem's lines with solid blocks of rectangular black" (Dworkin and Goldsmith 2011: 451). Levine does not photograph women or landscapes but rather pictures of them. It is her belief that we can only approach such subjects through their representation, "for what is offered to the gaze of the other is always a purloined image, a double or fake" (Owens 1992: 215). Subsequently, Hermann Zschiegner, an artist who participated in the *From Here On* exhibition (Fontcuberta 2013: 94–95), post-translates Levine's post-translation in a series of photography projects in the Google era. Thus, *+walkerevans+sherrielevine* is made up of twenty-six images of Allie Mae Burroughs that are the result of a Google search with the title of the series as a parameter. Levine is one of the most explicit examples of Gentzler's post-translation and of the outward turn: "[t]oday I suggest that all writing is rewriting, or better said, a rewriting of a rewriting of a rewriting, and translation . . . plays a significant role in that process" (Gentzler 2017: 10). In Levine, "copying becomes a new form of creativity; modifying a text becomes a new form of authorship" (Gentzler 2017: 14).

Thinking (and translating) *with* art (Chambers 2018: vi) is a pervasive theme throughout this book. Accordingly, art and translation are viewed as two critical and sometimes disturbing acts of meaning-making. Both are regarded as instigators of thinking which are more closely interrelated than previously thought. Translation and art can be defined as disciplines that are essentially restless and in movement[13] (Blanchot 1971/1976: 23). Different contemporary artistic languages have long discarded the outdated notion of borders between disciplines and of one absolute interpretation. The last chapter of this book shows that both in theory and practice, art has been aware for decades that it needs translation. In fact, many artistic manifestations are created from and with the idea of rewriting. Art is way ahead of translation when it comes to understanding the urgency of transgressing limits and boundaries between disciplines. It is thus possible to construct a(n) (in)definition of translation based on the novel reflections that art put forward decades ago on concepts such as the real, representation, the original, similarity, repetition, identity, margins, and many others.

Painting is a way of representing reality, of translating the real, in short, of rewriting. In *Ways of Seeing*, John Berger (1972) argues that between 1500 and 1900, what painting offered the viewer was one look, one translation of what the artist saw. It was a univocal homogeneous rewriting of the real that coincided with the patron's view of the world. In its origins, translation also offered univocal readings of the world. These readings, as seen in the colonial era, for example (evidenced by the studies of Vicente Rafael, Roberto Valdeón, Gayatri Spivak, Edward Said, Tejaswini Niranhana, Homi Bhabha, Marie-Louise Pratt, among others), painted the world according to the ideology of the person in charge of the translation. In contrast to this view of the world, the new looks of translation (Bassnett 2011, 2014a, 2017; Johnston 2013, 2017; Gentzler 2003, 2015, 2017; Lee 2013b, 2014a, 2014b, 2015a, 2015b, 2021b; Baynham and Lee 2019a, 2019b) point to a space that connects creative forms, initially far removed from each other, but which have strong links to the cultural practices they address. They can be regarded as a migration of signs between different formats, the change from one alphabet to another within dynamic referential frameworks, in constant transformation, always open to loans, resonances, and to blurred boundaries between genders and disciplines:

> Studies in semiotics suggest that the borders tend to be more multiple and permeable than traditionally conceived. What if we erase the border completely and rethink translation as an always ongoing process of *every* communication? Translation becomes viewed less as a speech-act carried out between languages and cultures, and instead as a condition underlying the languages and cultures upon which communication is based. This paper discusses research in translation, cultural studies, and semiotics and suggests a new model for translation studies, which includes related languages, overlapping sign systems, shared discourses, and multiple meanings.
>
> (Gentzler 2015: 1)

Gentzler's words perfectly summarize the aim of this book, which is to eliminate borders between disciplines, specifically between the world of art and translation with a view to implementing his new definition of translation, which transcends any boundaries between ways of representing the world. This all takes place "in a translation culture, or better said, translational cultures, always in an ongoing process of movement and maneuvering, invariably traversing boundaries, changing and adapting" (Gentzler 2017: 8). From this perspective, translation is no longer a secondary process but has become "one of the most important processes that can lead to revitalizing culture, a proactive force that continually introduces new ideas, forms or expressions, and pathways for change" (Gentzler 2017: 8).

This attitude favors translational or artistic creation understood as transliteration, in a world in which global symbols are asymmetrically exchanged between cultural mythologies that sometimes overlap and take advantage of positions of power. They reveal the urgency of looking at texts differently so that all meanings can be heard and all colors rewritten. Complicity between the various disciplines thus becomes an ethical question:

> The pursuit of thinking with artistic texts rather than generating and testing explanations is neither a retreat into abstractions that lack contact with the world nor an avoidance of ethical and political concerns. It is a practice of critique that should be understood both as a challenge to epistemological certainties and as a positive engagement with actual experiences and issues pertaining to them.
>
> (Shapiro 2013: xv)

This is reminiscent of Gertrude Stein's translations of Cézanne and Picasso's cubism, Kandinsky's translations of Schoenberg, Morton Feldman's musical translations of Abstract Expressionism, contemporary dance pieces that translate Stein (Aguiar and Queiroz 2015), Wayne McGregor's dance translations of Virginia Woolf's novels, and those well-known traditional ballets that translated Greek pastorals like *Daphnis and Chloe*, Shakespeare's plays such as *Romeo and Juliet*, novels like *Don Quixote*, and folktales like *Cinderella* and *Sleeping Beauty* (Bennett 2007). All these movement-based corporeal texts embody communication through kinesemiotics (Maiorani 2021) and translate previous originals outward by understanding dance as a language.

The translator, like the artist, has the power to create an image, and that image reflects his/her view. In other words, it reflects how s/he perceives what s/he translates, in the same way as the painter represents what s/he sees depending on his/her perspective or that of the person who has commissioned the painting. The methods used by the translator and painter to represent the original are many. In the case of the translator, they include the words chosen and their order as well as the nuances, connotations, smells (Grijelmo 2000), and noises (Vidal 2016). In the case of the painter, they encompass perspective, chiaroscuro, chromatic contrasts, figuration, abstraction, and the impressionist brushstroke. However, the important thing is that both paint spaces. The fact that the painter and translator have a variety of procedures to represent what they see is not a trivial matter. What is of interest here is that both must deal with problems related to the representation of origin and its implicit copy, how this representation is carried out, and the references used to do so.

In short, the question is how the translator establishes the relationship between words and things, how s/he does things with words, and how s/he looks at, paints, and listens to the world through translation. Since art has been asking these questions for centuries, this will help the translator to understand that representation is not imitation but interpretation. Blurring the boundaries between disciplines will help us understand translation

> as an ongoing process that is present in each communicative act, as an underlying condition for languages and cultures, able to resist particular social constructions, introduce new ideas, and question the status quo.
>
> (Gentzler 2017: 3)

We thus need new rules for new translation contexts if we want to understand, not only what the original text says, but *what the translation tells us*. This means understanding its processes, views, and perceptions of the outside world. Translation is a tool that moves between multiple conceptual and affective spheres, even when it moves within the contours of a single language. In this way we become aware of the contemporary need to write "the biography of translation" (Apter 2013: 266).

Writing the biography of translation signifies understanding translation as Paul Klee understood a drawing, a simple line that goes for a walk.

> When the translator takes a walk to that point through languages and cultures, what emerges is not a line drawing a fixed relationship between naked meanings but rather a kind of provisional mapping of that complex issue that is living. Thus, in the beginning was the word; but then translation took it for a walk.
>
> (Johnston 2017: 11)

Translation should be perceived as an instigator of mobility, as an opening to alterity, in a museum without walls like Malraux's, in a possible world where the original goes for a walk to suddenly become a surprisingly new image.

Translation is thus an inevitable process, one to which the human being is subjected from birth to death. Translating is interpreting. Every act of our existence is a translation, and our translations say a great deal about us. They betray us. They bring us closer to the other or take us away from them. In other words, they form us as human beings. We live translating, which means interpreting things into words and words into words. It is then when translation allows us to overcome the lethargy of our very self and becomes a stimulus, a creative process. "Translation as a form of writing, writing as a form of translation" (Bassnett 2011: 76). The translator as traveler (Bassnett 2004).

The first step would be to define translation from the look. Look to translate. Translate to look at the world. This means considering how images work. Images are visible ways of thinking, feeling, and, above all, ways of looking at the world. At the same time, my starting point is the fact that images speak to translate different realities. Images observe us and talk to us about their relationship with us, but they also speak of our relationship with them. Images touch the real (Didi-Huberman 2018). Translating from the translator's gaze or looking through our translations invites us to reflect on what images say when they speak (to us), on how words touch (us), on what words and images do, but above all what they do to us and what we do with them.

Indeed, on this journey outward, across borders, through entanglements that produce critical palimpsests, we seek to know what translation *does*. This means what its performative value is, how a text "communicates translational aliveness" (Apter 2006: 219). Translation can answer Mitchell's (2005) question about what images want, in that he treats them almost as living beings. Translating with art will reveal what the text says without saying. It will show the walls that others have built, walls that are sometimes obvious, but which, on other occasions (the most dangerous) are not visible. By thinking through/with images, the translator will also think of the form and context in which these images are immersed and thus go beyond "the Kantian pact that guarantees the sovereignty of the Occidental subject" and the fact that the others "refuse to be othered" (Chambers 2014: 244). In that sense, images "point to a relational and constructed reality" (Guasch 2016: 352). Translating with art will allow us to counteract essentialisms and binary oppositions. Translating in motion taking images into account will create spaces for dialogue and debate, *donner langue* to be able to

> learn and relearn how to *see* the world, how to *live* in the world, how to *behave* in the world. Maybe we should remember that our art forges tools for change and constitutes objects encapsulating change, that it indicates ways of becoming other and making other; and as well that our art is perhaps a way of losing possession of useless certainties.
> (Breytenbach 2009: 17)

Translation thus becomes a way of giving back to the other the right to look.[14]

Notes

1. "Vision is a cultural construction . . . it is learned and cultivated, not simply given by nature . . . It is deeply involved with human societies, with the ethics and politics, aesthetics and epistemology of seeing and being seen" (Mitchell 2002: 166).
2. "Visual culture involves the things that we see, the mental model we all have of how to see, and what we can do as a result. That is why we call it *visual culture*: a culture of the visual. A visual culture is not simply the total amount of what has been made to be seen, such as paintings or films. A visual culture is the relation between what is visible and the names that we give to what is seen. It also involves what is invisible or kept out of sight. In short, we don't simply see what there is to see and call it a visual culture. Rather, we assemble a worldview that is consistent with what we know and have already experienced" (Mirzoeff 2016: 10).
3. Contemporary languages on signs in the public domain "include greater contextual (ethnographic) and historical understandings of texts in the landscape—who put them there, how they are interpreted, and what role they play in relation to space, migration and mobility" (Pennycook 2017: 270), because these signs are in many cases multilingual, as shown by Pennycook's ethnographic observation at a Bangladeshi-owned corner shop in Sydney, where not only words but the distribution of space, objects, goods, food, and other "semiotic assemblages" turned the whole situation into a translingual cosmopolitan space.
4. From the definitions of Brinker, Halliday and Hasan, De Beaugrande and Dressler, Van Dijk or Petöfi, among others, we have reached those of scholars who, based on the semiosis of Charles S. Peirce, understand that the text is an interdisciplinary or transdisciplinary concept and consequently includes nonverbal phenomena, images, and culturally specific visual or musical references. Since the 1960s onward, the concept of "text" "has been redefined and reconceptualized to include meaning structures comprised of varying semiotic codes" (Desjardins 2008: 48).
5. Some artists urge us to look at cities through the lens of translation—for instance Canan Marasligil, herself a translator, in her project *City in Translation*, based on the traces people leave in urban spaces (Lee 2021a). In fact, when Iain Chambers refers to "the grammar of the city", he does so in terms of translation. In this regard, he defines the city as "a translating and translated space" since language is always a plural concept, not merely a linguistic matter. Architecture, music, painting, dance are ways to speak "in the vicinity of other histories and cultures, proximate to others who may refuse our terms of translation" (Chambers 2018: 33).
6. A good example of this venue is the excellent series on multimodality at Routledge, edited by Kay O'Halloran which aims "to advance knowledge of multimodal resources such as language, visual images, gesture, action, music, sound, 3-D artefacts, architecture and space, as well as the ways these resources integrate to create meaning in multimodal objects and events" (web page).

7. As is well-known, the interrelationships between literature and painting based on *ut pictura poesis* and ekphrasis have been widely explored (e.g., Venuti 2010; Bal 1991; Drucker 1997; Krieger 1991; Hollander 1995; Robillard and Jongeneel 1998). Other publications include *The Sister Arts* (1958) by Jean H. Hagstrum, *The Color of Rhetoric* (1982) by Wendy Steiner, *Pictoria Concepts* (1989) by Göran Sonneson, *The Gazer's Spirit: Poems Speaking to Silent Works of Art* (1995) by John Hollander, and *La imagen compleja. La fenomenología de las imágenes en la era de la cultura visual* (2005) by Josep Catalá.

8. For instance, "Transmedial Turn? Potentials, Problems and Points to Consider", 8–11 December 2020, University of Tartu, Estonia. This second conference in a series of academic gatherings dedicated to the study of intersemiotic processes in culture concentrated on "the cultural shift from logocentric to increasingly intersemiotic, intermedial and transmedial processes and in its impact on disciplines that study textual transfers, relations between semiotic systems or media and new media practices" (https://transmedia.ut.ee/). It is also worth mentioning that such institutions as The Center for Translation Studies at the University of Texas have offered a transdisciplinary approach to translation for decades.

9. On the ETN website at the following link: https://experientialtranslation.net/

10. Arlene Tucker's artistic project *Translation Is Dialogue: Language in Transit (TID)* applies Torop's approach to translation: see Campbell and Vidal 2019: xxxvi.

11. The multimodal perspective draws on the concept of social semiotics that derives from Halliday and his functional view of language and, from his ideas, the multimodal social semiotic approaches generated by Kress (2003, 2010), van Leeuwen (2021), Kress and van Leeuwen (1996, 2001), Bezemer and Kress (2016), Jewitt (2009), Jewitt *et al.* (2016) among others. Contemporary meanings are best dealt with through the semiotic category of mode (Kress in Boria *et al.* 2020: 47).

12. Madeleine Campbell has written about translation as "exhausting" the possibilities of the rhizome, drawing a parallel with Beckett's instructions for the Quad dance piece: https://ir.uiowa.edu/poroi/vol13/iss1/2/

13. Blanchot dedicates the fifth chapter of *The Laughter of the Gods* (1971/1976) to translation, which he understands as an *original* activity by translators, whom he calls "writers" (Blanchot 1971/1976: 54, 55 and 57). Classical Works "are only alive because they are translated" (*ibid.*: 57), but above all he points out that translation does not erase but is based on difference, "it is the very essence of difference" (*ibid.*: 56).

14. The right to look, according to Nicholas Mirzoeff (2011a, 2011b), or, on the other hand, the right not to be looked at, as advocated by Kevin Coleman (2015).

2   The Artistranslator's Gaze

2.1 Looking

Looking is a way of narrating the world, and thus a way to translate it. Not surprisingly, Marcel Proust said that the real journey is not about walking along a path but about having new eyes. But how to look? How to use your eyes (Elkins 2000)? Who is the subject who looks when s/he sees him/herself reflected in another? How does the person who looks understand that fracture when s/he is being looked at? Or vice versa. Indeed, our way of looking at the other not only reveals a great deal about who we are. It also explains the images and words we choose to narrate and paint reality.

We are living not only in heteroglossic times but also in multifaceted cultures. Images have also narrated terror.[1] Different ways of looking at the world give rise to clashes when it comes to representing and seeing difference.[2] Today, neither nations nor individuals are one-dimensional, hence the need to not only propose new ways of seeing and looking, but also to rewrite those looks, because what we have are not so much facts as representations (Mitchell 2005). "Looking, seeing, and knowing have become perilously intertwined" (Jencks *et al.* 1995: 1, 2).

In the 1990s, Western society began to take the first steps toward what we know today as the image society. Creating and sending images of all kinds, from photographs to videos, comics, art, and animation, is extremely commonplace as reflected in statistics:

> One of the most notable uses of the global network is to create, send, and view images of all kinds, from photographs to video, comics, art, and animation. The numbers are astonishing: three hundred hours of YouTube video are uploaded every minute. Six billion hours of video are watched every month on the site, one hour for every person on earth. The 18–34 age group watches more YouTube than cable television. (And remember that YouTube was only created in 2005). Every

two minutes, Americans alone take more photographs than were made in the entire nineteenth century. . . . Like it or not, the emerging global society is visual. All these photographs and videos are our way of trying to see the world. We feel compelled to make images of it and share them with others as a key part of our effort to understand the changing world around us and our place within it.

(Mirzoeff 2016: 4, 5)

From McLuhan's global village, we have shifted, beyond the society of the spectacle, to the iconosphere, where we inhabit the image while the image inhabits us. This confirms the omens of Debord and the situationists, particularly with the implementation of digital technology and social networks, which circulate images at high speed and have transformed their performative role. Images can be both active and dangerous. Their number has multiplied exponentially, and they are much more difficult to control than in the non-digital era (Fontcuberta 2016: 7ff).

At this time social sciences and the humanities are shifting their lines of research toward the visual, as reflected in the standard bibliography on visual culture and its venues (Bryson and Bal 1991; Bryson *et al.* 1994; Jencks 1995; Evans and Hall 1999; Barnard 2001; Elkins 2012; Heywood and Sandywell 2011; Moxey 2008; Smith 2005, 2008; Dovitskaya 2005; Sturken and Cartwright 2009; Mirzoeff 1998, 1999, 2011a, 2016), visual grammars in the visual language of comics (Cohn 2013, 2018), and cultural differences in visual languages. The same thing is occurring in other fields such as anthropology (Appadurai 1988; Pink 2006, 2007; Pinney 2011) or methodology (Rose 2001/2007). This highlights the urgency of what Emily Apter (2007: 152) in Translation Studies calls converting "the reading into the looking . . . the looking as a mode of resistant reading". Expanding the definition of translation to incorporate the image as a constructed sign that communicates and thus must be translated means considering the "commitment to look" (Bal 2005). This broadening of horizons will make us aware of how things become visible, what becomes visible and why:

what is made visible? (And what is rendered invisible?) How is it made visible, exactly—what technologies are used, and how. . . . And what are the effects of those visualized materialities and materialized visualities, particularly for the people caught up in those practices . . . it is only through such engagements with visual and material culture that we stand a chance of understanding just how contemporary culture is once again reshaping and reforming itself.

(Rose and Tolia-Kelly 2012: 9)

It is important to reflect on the urgency of translating to see, of seeing and looking to translate, and of being aware of the power relations generated between two texts, between sign systems of any kind. Equally relevant is how institutions, who cling to certain ways of seeing and ordering the world, cause them to prevail so that other views do not seem to be possible (Haraway 1991). In the global era,

> the emergence of the Internet as a digital and visual storage medium and the overproduction of pictures and images in our media society—all hint at an iconic turn. . . . Yet talk of an iconic turn is not just a reference to the increasing importance of visual phenomena of everyday culture. This turn has led to a new epistemological awareness of images in the study of culture. Linked to a critique of knowledge and language, it seeks to promote a visual literacy that has been poorly developed in Western societies since Plato's hostility toward images and logocentrist trends in philosophy. The dominance of language in Western cultures has long marginalized the study of visual cultures.
>
> (Bachmann-Medick 2016b: 245)

Images create "l'effet de réel" (Barthes 1968), bringing to light "the ideological, epistemological, and representational implications of dominating modes of vision, including their illusory monopoly in the domain of display" (Bal 1996: 8). Images "do not circulate without purpose . . . They are produced by cultures and societies, nations and states, they not only serve as messengers, but they also transmit essential components of their cultural, social, and national identities" (Mersmann and Schneider 2009: 1). Images are constructed for political, economic, and ideological purposes. The profusion of images is supported not only by the media and markets but also by official institutions and organizations through the omnipresence of a series of miraculous devices that are post-technological eyes that have made the impossible possible. They embody the look of the non-subject who gazes at us, and range from divine omnipresence, symbolized in Christianity by an open eye without an eyelid, inscribed in a triangle representing the Trinity, to Galileo's optical telescope. Today we have spy satellites and video surveillance cameras, which are the new divine eyes that are equally omnipresent, this time in public space. However, we have no shame in exhibiting our privacy, what Lacan called *extimicy*, on social networks (Fontcuberta 2016).

In that iconic avalanche, we ourselves are often images (Fontcuberta 2017), images of all kinds that summarize in digital code the two most traditional genres in the history of art, the self-portrait and vanity, encapsulated today in a huge variety of selfies (from the most innocent to the most exhibitionist: Fontcuberta *et al.* 2010). A selfie is nothing but a self-translation.

It "depicts the drama of our own daily performance of ourselves" (Mirzoeff 2016: 30). Contrary to the traditional autobiography, this image is a text that reflects and is reflected in the narcissistic surface of the mirror and in the Baudrillardian full screen of the mobile phone. Nevertheless, as in any self-translation, the new text, which is an image, does not say the same as the original. As Umberto Eco (2003) would argue, the original and its reflection say *quasi la stessa cosa*, almost the same thing. It is an autobiography that reveals a great deal about us, our nothingness, our liquid self, to quote Bauman (2000), but it does not say everything.

This is how we tell ourselves today, how we introduce ourselves and exhibit ourselves, how we self-narrate through images. However, images may also be a way to hide our true self in this era of digital surfaces, where the image on networks is far from real, where we look and are looked at, trying perhaps to control the darker side of oculocentrism.

2.2 The Image as a Constructed Text

The frenzy of images leads to a hypervisibility and voyeurism that is worth analyzing, especially because of the dangerous consequences of how these images are managed, disseminated, and controlled in our society, as artists like Antoni Muntadas in his projects on translation have warned (Vidal in press). It is, in short, a question of the translator looking from that new line of research, long assumed by the art world, which arises from the belief that images can constitute political criticism or a way of manipulating those who look at them.

This research venue (based on the early work of an American pioneer, W.J.T. Mitchell and his *Iconology: Image, Text, Ideology*, 1986) stems from two intellectual traditions namely, French post-structuralism and British cultural studies (led by Raymond Williams, Fredric Jameson, and Stuart Hall). These scholars and many others highlight the political and constructed dimension of the image as a text that communicates (Rose and Tolia-Kelly 2012) and determines the right to look (Mirzoeff 2011a, 2011b).

The constructed nature of images forces the viewer to reflect on the diversity and inequality of those who are looked at. In this venue, John Berger (1972) asked many years ago if the way in which we look affects what we know. And Roland Barthes emphasized that every image, like words, brings with it that secondary level of meaning, which is really what must be translated. Nevertheless, it is also the most difficult to rewrite because that is where translators are most exposed, where the words that they choose betray them:

> In front of a photograph, the feeling of "denotation", or, if one prefers, of analogical plenitude, is so great that the description of a photograph

is literally impossible; *to describe* consists precisely in joining to the denoted message a relay or second-order message derived from a code which is that of language and constituting in relation to the photographic analogue, however much care one takes to be exact, a connotation: to describe is thus not simply to be imprecise or incomplete, it is to change structures, to signify something different to what is shown.

(Barthes 1977: 18–19)

In fact, Barthes' photographer is in the same dilemma as the translator. Every image, like every translated text, embodies a way of seeing. Every time we look at a photograph, we are aware that the photographer, who rewrote reality through his look, chose that image from an endless number of other possible images. Furthermore, our perception of an image also depends on our own way of seeing, as pointed out by John Berger (1972) in his book of three pictorial essays, written with images, and four verbal essays, painted with words. Berger argues that "seeing comes before words", that "seeing establishes our place in the surrounding world" and that "the relation between what we see and what we know is never settled" (Berger 1972: 7).

As Fabbri (2017) would say, communication does not occur between identical subjects but between subjects who have their own codes and subcodes. "The way we see things is affected by what we know or what we believe. . . . We never look at just one thing; we are always looking at the relation between things and ourselves" (Berger 1972: 8, 9). Communication is not a transparent cooperative process, but also has to do with what is silenced, with what is hidden, and with what is implicit. "Every image embodies a way of seeing" (Berger 1972: 10). And it is precisely the look that scrutinizes (the one that decides to look from another perspective) that the outward translator finds interesting:

photographs are not, as is often assumed, mechanical records. Every time we look at a photograph, we are aware, however slightly, of the photographer selecting that sight from an infinity of other possible sights. This is true even in the most family snapshot. The photographer's way of seeing is reflected in his choice of the subject. The painter's way of seeing is reconstituted by the marks he makes on the canvas or paper. Yet, although every image embodies a way of seeing, our perception or appreciation of an image depends also on our way of seeing.

(Berger 1972: 10)

Reality is accessed from the right and obligation to look. This is a political claim because it is not only related to our rights, but also to those of others (Mulvey 1975, 1989/2009; Jay 1993).

After Richard Rorty's linguistic turn (1967), there was a return to the image in the eighties. In 1992 William J.T. Mitchell speaks of the "pictorial turn", and in 1994, Gottfried Boehm of the "iconic turn".[3] Mitchell, explaining his "pictorial turn" in his now canonical *Picture Theory*, argues that "we live in a world of images" (1994: 41), and that the problems of the twenty-first century will be the problems of the image. He underlines the fact that everything is transformed into images, and that what is consumed is in the form of an image. Mitchell understands the pictorial turn as a post-linguistic rediscovery of the image. For him, it is a concept that crosses through a wide variety of research fields, since there is an "inextricable weaving together of representation and discourse" (Mitchell 1994: 83).

He does not suggest giving more importance to the visual than the verbal, but he insists that we understand the interactions between visual and verbal representations as well as their relations with the broader cultural issues. In his opinion, in a society which has surrendered to visual simulations, stereotypes, copies, and reproductions, the image constructs reality and produces meaning. In short, it communicates. It is a way of translating reality.

There are no purely visual media. All arts are composed (both text and image), and they combine different discursive conventions, channels, and sensory and cognitive modes: "the interaction of pictures and texts is constitutive of representation as such: all media are mixed media, and all representations are heterogeneous; there are no 'purely' visual or verbal arts" (Mitchell 1994: 5). That is why Mitchell does not oppose both turns nor does he consider that the linguistic turn is replaced or opposed by the pictorial turn. Hence, based on Michel Foucault's analysis of *Las Meninas* by Velázquez, Mitchell points out in *Picture Theory* that the relationship between language and painting is infinite, and distinguishes between *image/ text, image-text* and *imagetext*.

Imagetext refers to the fact that contemporary representation does not arise from a rupture or a simple relationship between the categories of image and text, but rather from their interrelation. "I will employ the typographic convention of the slash to designate 'image/text' as a problematic gap, cleavage, or rupture in representation. The term 'imagetext' designates composite, synthetic works (or concepts) that combine image and text. 'Image-text', with a hyphen, designates relations of the visual and the verbal" (Mitchell 1994: 89). This makes it also possible to envisage a "readerviewer" or even a "readerviewertranslator". What is important about Mitchell's new categorization is that for him, imagetexts are not only aesthetic but are also motivated by interventions in the semi-political sphere of a certain medium (Mitchell 1994: 91). The image transforms the framework in which it is inscribed into "a site of conflict, a nexus where political, institutional, and social antagonisms play themselves out in the materiality of representation" (*id.*).

In this context, Gottfried Boehm's "iconic turn" (used for the first time in his 1994 anthology, *What Is an Image?*) is a useful concept. Both turns, that of Mitchell and Boehm, arise almost simultaneously to give greater prominence to the image, though Boehm's is based more on anthropology and the philosophy of language. In a letter to Mitchell, Boehm states that

> the question about the image touches the foundation of culture and poses new challenges for science. Because the "image" is not simply a new topic, but rather implies another type of thinking, a thinking that is able to clarify and take advantage of the cognitive possibilities to be found in nonverbal representations . . . the image is not as innocent or as immediate as the eye because it is connected in multiple ways with intellectual, discursive, cultural, ideological and gender contexts.
>
> (Boehm 2011: 59)

That is why he wishes to construct a "hermeneutics of the image" in reference to Gadamerian hermeneutics, which, far from being limited to language, understands that it is a dimension capable of encompassing manifestations of meaning through music, dance, and image. Boehm (*ibid.*: 66) thus suggests "a mutual translation" between the visible and the sayable:

> It is not at all about completely isolating images from language, but it is based on the fact that linguistic communication is able to decode images. To this end, I have used the model of a mutual translation, which not only points to the discourse on images, but in return makes it possible to verify whether a word "has hit the mark" when contrasted with the original, that is, with the image [my translation].

Boehm's 1994 anthology was his first attempt at researching language in relation to its implicit deictic power. His intention was to expand the linguistic turn toward the iconic turn to provide nonverbal visual logic with a verifiable argumentative form.

What we see depends "upon where you were when" (Berger 1972: 18). Every image is the story of a look at something. Picasso's owl (1947) is not merely any owl, but the story of a specific human being who looks at an owl in a certain way. In the same way, Joseph Kosuth's chair(s) in his *One and Three Chairs* (1965) is an interpretation of the chair among many others. In other words, every image "presents a personal perspective of reality" (Hockney and Gayford 2016: 8). For this reason, we must ask ourselves how we see what we see, who put it there for us to see, and what these images show and from what point of view.

As observed by Roland Barthes, forms of representation are necessarily historical.

> The code of connotation was in all likelihood neither "natural" nor "artificial" but historical, or, if it be preferred, "cultural". Its signs are gestures, attitudes, expressions, colors or effects, endowed with certain meanings by virtue of the practice of a certain society: the link between signifier and signified remains if not unmotivated, at least entirely historical.
>
> (Barthes 1977: 27)

In this same line, Mitchell relates the subjectivity of the look to the social circumstances that affect us when it comes to perceiving the world. In his view, the look is understood as a cultural construction that has to do with ethics, politics, and the epistemology of seeing and being seen, of how we look and at whom:

> it is the realization that *spectatorship* (the look, the gaze, the glance, the practices of observation, surveillance, and visual pleasure) may be as deep a problem as various forms of *reading* (decipherment, decoding, interpretation) and that visual experience or "visual literacy" might not be fully explicable on the model of textuality.
>
> (Mitchell 1994: 16)

That is why Mitchell highlights the constructed nature of images:

> [V]ision and visual images, things that (to the novice) are apparently automatic, transparent, and natural, are actually symbolic constructions, like a language to be learned, a system of codes that interposes an ideological veil between us and the real world. This overcoming of what has been called the natural attitude has been crucial to the elaboration of visual studies as an arena for political and ethical critique, and we should not underestimate its importance.
>
> (Mitchell 2002: 170–171)

This is similar to Bachmann-Medick (2016b: 259) on the concept of image in translation studies. "The recognition that all images, even photographs, are constructed, produced and configured, if only because of the selection of details and focuses, reinforces doubts about authentic representations and authenticity as a whole".

2.3 Images in Translation Studies

We live immersed in multiple and different semiotic environments,[4] a term used in the same way as in Umberto Eco's *Trattato di semiotica generale* (1975).[5] Accordingly, to do their job, translators not only have to *read* but also *look, listen, touch,* and *feel.* The contemporary world has greatly expanded forms of communication. This makes it necessary to speak of languages (in the plural) as systems of representation that both construct meaning and transmit it. It is thus imperative to expand the traditional definition of translation "to encompass a wide range of activities and products that do not necessarily involve an identifiable relationship with a discrete source" (Baker 2014: 15).

A semiotic perspective on meaning challenges our approach to translating (Marais 2019). Such a perspective not only considers *how* translations represent but also the *effects* and consequences of that representation. It is a question of "not only how language and representation produce meaning, but how the knowledge which a particular discourse produces connects with power, regulates conduct, makes up or constructs identities and subjectivities, and defines the way certain things are represented" (Hall 1997/2003: 6). To achieve this, translators should remember that globalization has produced specific sign-making practices within fragmented and diverse communities that do not necessarily share a common cultural background. Within this changing, transnational semiotic landscape, translators are obliged to reflect on what type of language they are translating. They should also be aware of the context; for whom the text was created and why; and also in which cultural community or group the text arose. Evidently, meaning is a slippery customer. It is neither static nor transparent but rather depends on its representation and on the surroundings in which it is generated (Mirzoeff 2011a; Hall 1997/2003; Rose 2001/2007; Berger 1972).

When the translator views translation as a situated and situating multidirectional activity, the focus shifts

> toward artistic productions, as they frequently constitute cultural and media composites. In these composites, there is an interplay between not just different languages and their modal forms of expression, but also between different media articulations, between image, tone, and sound, between material installation, a given spatial ambience, and patterns of reception, and between configurations of protagonists and viewers.
>
> (Ott and Weber 2019: 8)

The relation between verbality and visuality in multimodal literary art, the analysis of a "radically different linguistic order, where verbal texts are functionally taken over by visual signs" (Lee 2014a: 43), is a new and important research venue that some scholars have already taken in the field of Translation Studies (Lee 2011, 2013b, 2014a, 2014b, 2015a, 2015b).

Translation is expanding

> to become a central action perspective in a complex environment, one that can be applied to all forms of intercultural contact, the establishment of links between disciplines, and methodologically enhanced comparative approaches informed by a new view of cultural comparisons.
>
> (Bachmann-Medick 2016b: 175–176)

Translation is "a model for connecting disciplines" (Bachmann-Medick 2016b: 189). It is a vehicle for new ways of seeing, of listening, and of being in a cosmopolitan world that generates a way of translating that threatens established models that have proved to be unsuitable for our contemporary hybrid transnational society. The translator now has to bear in mind that

> in all these elaborate cycles of dominance and contestation of dominance and the complex interplay between power and resistance, some form of translation is almost always present. This has always been the case, but it is particularly true of the twenty-first century, with its globalized economies and aggressive resurgence of colonial empires. . . . But we must remember that translation also offers—and has always offered—major opportunities for contesting and undermining this very domination.
>
> (Baker 2006: 25)

This way of translating understands that "text" is a very broad concept made up of many types of semiotic system. The translator lives in a world that is in permanent flux, in a universe that dances with "the terrible spaces of dispossession", where the individual is in constant movement. This is vividly described by Breyten Breytenbach (2009: n.p.), a poet who inhabits that "middle world" where "he reflects, and then he encircles with words the things seen".

In today's world, this translating activity is metaphorical, dancing among all types of signs and revealing

> its capacity to serve as a vehicle for new ways of seeing and being that enable us to question the received ideas that structure the worlds in which we live. My argument is that it is through "text" in its broadest understanding—through the traditions, inscriptions and institutions of

culture and society—that we communicate our being in the world. In a hermeneutic sense, to "read" the world as if it were a text is to understand something of how our being is constructed and what this implies about being alive.

(Maitland 2017: n.p.)

2.4 The Translator's Gaze

Emily Apter (2007: 149) very aptly raises the need to challenge "the word-based model of 'the reading', by translating 'the reading' into the lookings". She emphasizes the importance of looking to translate the world and proposes a shift from a word-based model of translation to one that is based on translating by reading what one looks at. This model consists of looking to read and translating by looking. More than a decade ago, Apter had already gone one step beyond Jakobson's intersemiotic translation and described such translation as a journey along and across the boundaries of disciplines. On this journey, we learn to see and look at the multiple layers that construct images and words. This teaches us that communication "happens on many levels, the gestural, the olfactory, the visual, the linguistic" (Campbell and Vidal 2019: xxv), because as Benjamin points out in "The Task of the Translator" (1968), communication with words is only one very concrete example of human language.

With Fabbri and Lotman, we start from the idea that translation does not occur exclusively between verbal sign systems but also between verbal and nonverbal signs. Fabbri (2012) reveals that translation is a form of conflict, a battlefield where the meaning of the signs around us is negotiated. Far from negative, it is a way to generate new meanings and approaches between cultures because the important thing is not the static sign itself, but rather the procedures used to endow the sign with meanings. It is thus urgent to address Lotman's semiosphere, which Fabbri mentions. In this semiosphere, translation is a constant activity because it is a multimedia, multimodal space. Awareness of the semiotic project of globalization means understanding the translation activities produced by the semiosphere.

In this context, there are promising initiatives (i.e., Didi-Huberman 2018; Campbell and Vidal 2019), that define the translator's gaze as that look that uses the eyes, as well as the whole body to understand:

> *The translator's gaze*, the intense engagement of the translator with the source text which also entails an appropriation of sorts—not just with the eyes but with all other senses. . . . Perceiving through the eyes, ears, tongue or body of another opens the willing recipient (performer or spectator) to unfamiliar affects and sensory experiences, a

"disorienting" event that can, if enacted in a safe environment, lead to personal growth and greater levels of awareness and understanding of the other, and thereby enhance cultural literacy.

(Campbell and Vidal 2019: xxix, xxxiv)

This entails moving from language to consider "the materiality and affordances of the visual, of gesture, and the body in order to communicate, takes translanguaging into the intersemiotic, multimodal domain" (Baynham and Lee 2019a: 97; see also Lee 2014b). The reader may engage the text in translation, "not primarily affectively, but physically and sensuously" (Lee 2014b: 348). For instance, Sam Treadaway uses his nose to translate Simon Barraclough's concrete poem "Two sun spots" as "Sniff Disc",[6] a tightly printed disc of intensely scented paper fitted in an opaque sleeve. Printed in the shape of several expanding circles, the original poem is extremely visual, yet Treadaway's translation results in a poem that can be smelled:

> Each line is converted into a drop of a particular essential oil, but in the final scent, all of them are mixed together, transforming the overall atmosphere of the poem into one olfactory sensation. Apprehending "Sniff Disc" requires the primarily visual act of reading, as described above, to become a primarily physical act. As a reader of Treadaway's work, we need to literally unpack the poem, moving from the outside in, first the cover, past the song lines (names of scents) on the sleeve towards the disc. At this stage, reading entails an obvious physical immersion: as one literally plunges one's nose into the centre of the poem, the visual disappears behind the olfactory experience. While Treadaway's work is as multimodal as Barraclough's original poem, it is now the sensorial, and in particular the olfactory, modality that is the most overwhelming aspect. Treadaway's intersemiotic translation foregrounds the creative qualities of both reading and translation: it exposes the work involved in communication and shows the potential of translation to go beyond the act of carrying across.
>
> Treadaway's translation of the poem into scent . . . presented on a 3-D object foregrounds the material and sensorial modalities.

(Campbell and Vidal 2019: 14)

This translation, from the visual into the olfactory, exemplifies Campbell and Vidal's (2019: xxv) idea that "communication happens on many levels". It shows that not only words communicate—we read and we see with all our senses.[7]

Using digital photography and computer code to translate a poem by Denise Riley, Treadaway also contributed a multimodal translation to

Translation Games: Still in Translation[8] (curated by Ricarda Vidal and Maria-José Blanco 2015). An artist book including artwork, poetry, and translations, made by Vidal as final output of the project, can also be considered an example of an expanded definition of translation:

> Denise Riley's unpublished poem *Still* provided the source text for the game . . . the poem was given to an artist [Treadaway] with the commission to translate the words into imagery. The artist passed on their image (but not the original text) to another artist asking them to translate into another image, which was passed on to the next artist. In this way the work was translated through a chain of 12 artists, each working with the medium of their choice and each producing an original translation of the work created by the previous artist in the chain. They could use any medium as long as the work could be depicted as a digital still image. We also asked each artist to provide us and the next person in the chain with a brief commentary on their translation. The final image was subject to a poetry competition in which participants were asked to retranslate the work into words. Finally, and with recourse to all the different versions of "Still", Maria-José and Ricarda produced literary translations of "Still" into Spanish and German.

Also relevant is *Revolve: R* (Arrow Bookworks and Intellect 2018), edited by Sam Treadaway and Ricarda Vidal, a bookart project which is a practice-based exploration of visual communication:

> an artwork image is sent to artists around the world (UK, USA, Africa and Continental Europe) with an invitation to respond and reply with a work of their own. After each artist has submitted a response, a second artwork image is produced and returned to all participating artists as a remix, edit and synthesis of the collected artwork material.
>
> This process is repeated six times, producing the six chapters (or *Revolves*) of this lavishly produced, limited-edition bookwork. With a focus on experimentation, exchange and creative development the project models communications between international arts communities and transcends geographic and linguistic boundaries (www. revolve-r.com).

Vidal's artist book *Still in Translation* was part of *TransARTation! Wandering Texts, Travelling Objects* (2017),[9] a touring and virtual exhibition of inter-art translation curated by Manuela Perteghella, Eugenia Loffredo, and Anna Milsom and funded by Arts Council England. This exhibition shows Apter's translating idea of translating "the reading" into "the lookings". It shows the interactions among words, moving and still images and translation. In the catalogue, translation is described as "a transdisciplinary activity, drawing upon and contributing to a whole range of ideas and practices that include, but can go far beyond, taking a text from one language into another" (in Andrews 2018: 32). Behind this exhibition we find "[t]he formal translational (transductive) moves from word to image, image to word" (*id.*). One of the artists, Kirsteen Anderson, plays with the way visual and verbal texts "intertranslate" each other, and Ira Lightman offers a visual translation of Apollinaire (*ibid.*: 32–34). Another excellent example is a Bittersuite concert, during which the performers translate sound into spectators' bodies through touch.[10]

Caroline Bergvall also interests us here particularly because "she takes the semantic to be produced both aurally and visually" (Perloff 2004: 42). She creates performable performance pieces, text-based performances[11] and works interested in cross-media and site-related approaches to writing. Bergvall is concerned with art and writing that have to do with "ways of looking at things, ways of applying oneself to a reading of the world" (Bergvall 2000: 50). She creates "writerly" works (in the Barthian sense) which challenge accepted norms of readability and accessibility. All her work is about the complex relationship between linguistic translation and spatial translation engaging in notions of space, body (*Eclat, Fig, Flèsh Acoeur*[12], *Flèsh*), sense, voice (*Ambient Fish, Your Say I Moved*), language, silence (*Words and Silence*, a poetry performance in the John Ashbery Poetry Series at Bard College), multilingualism and translation. In fact, she defines translation

> as a field which allows for the text in the original language to force up an activity of writing and exchange in the translation language. By which I mean one which almost certainly diffuses and stretches the arrival language. Making strange language which reveals the "other" text, the "foreign" language across the familiarity of the arrival language. Sets up the two languages in conflictual or dialogic relationality.
> (Bergvall 2000: 51)

For Bergvall, language is "a physical and bodily experience" (Rabourdin 2020: 58), thus the central role of breathing in her performances.

Translation is preset in her collection of poems *Fig*. For instance, "Via", both a text and a sound piece that arranges translations alphabetically, is about "Making copy explicitly as an act of copy" (Bergvall 2005: 65), so it can be understood as a post-translation:

> Through the simple act of transcribing and cataloguing, Bergvall forces the texts to reveal themselves in ways that would be impossible through

a more traditional close reading or elucidation. By doing less—almost nothing, really— she is doing more, reminding us that a strategy of mere reframing is a strong and effective way of conceptual writing.

(Dworkin and Goldsmith 2011: 81)

On the other hand, in the installation piece "Say: 'Parsley'" the opposite happens. While "Via" is a collection of translations of an Italian text by Dante through which Bergvall "is acting as a sort of translator by simply recasting preexisting texts into a new poem that is entirely her own" (Goldsmith 2011: 194), "Say: 'Parsley'" takes as its starting point "a finite body of English words so as to understand their potential for *translation*, whether into the various idiolects and dialects circulating in the United Kingdom or in the warring speech registers of Belgium, specifically Flemish-speaking Antwerp, where English has replaced French as a second language of choice" (Perloff 2010: 131). The work consists of a printed version, a series of installations, and a digital version with sound/screen on the Internet, and in all of them "translation and translatability are viewed in political as well as poetic terms" (Perloff 2010: 131). Bergvall reflects on the implications of pronouncing a word in one way or another, about what others think of someone who does not pronounce "correctly". In fact, the installation begins with the words "how you speak will be used against you", and continues with a series of people who repeat the same phrase, "rolling hills", again and again. However, what the artist seems to want to convey to us is that the phrase is never the same, since the accent and the way of saying changes with each visitor, and thus, the phrase is neither original nor repetition, but both at the same time. The presentation of this installation for the Jewish Museum (Munich 2019) says the following:

"Say Parsley" is a sparse sound and language installation which exposes the power of language to single out and denunciate speakers. In the wake of official and brutal unofficial responses in the UK to 9/11, this felt particularly acute. Working with composer Ciaran Maher allowed a subtle and spatial exploration of psychoacoustic events that all inform processes of mishearings, misrecognition, assumptions, and misattribution. *You hear what you want to hear. You hear what you think you hear.*

The background to "Say Parsley" is the biblical "shibboleth", a violent event where language itself is gatekeeper, and a pretext to massacre. The pronunciation of a given word exposes the identity of the speaker. *To speak becomes a give-away. Are you one of us, not one of us? How you speak will be used against you.* The most recent example of a large-scale shibboleth was the massacre of tens of thousands of Creole Haitians on the border of the Dominican Republic in 1937, when the criteria for execution was the failure to pronounce "perejil" (parsley) in the accepted Spanish manner, with a rolling "r".

With the pronunciation of a single word the origin of the person who says it is detected: the voice is political, the original and its repetition can have ideological connotations. Bergvall focusses on expressions like "parsley" or "rolling hills", which are easy for English speakers to pronounce but not, for example, for the Japanese who have difficulty pronouncing the European style /r/), and this reminds us that language can be a form of discrimination:

> Speaking is a give-away. My tongue marks me out. It also trips me up, creates social stuttering, mishearing, ambiguities . . . In the culturally pluralistic, yet divided, and markedly monolingual society of contemporary Britain, variations in accent and deviations from a broad English pronunciation still frequently entail degrees of harassment and verbal, sometimes physical, abuse, all according to ethnic and linguistic background.
>
> (Bergvall in Perloff 2010: 131–132)

Bergvall envisages foreignness, difference, through a spatial reflection on sound. She juxtaposes languages in order to question the stability of a language, its authenticity, its originality. In her installation, linguistic displacement is a sign of resistance. In the printed version of "Say: 'Parsley'" that was presented at the Museum of Contemporary Art in Antwerp in 2008, she played again with translation and multilingualism, with the phonetic translations of English words into Flemish (for a detailed explanation of this interesting installation, see Perloff 2004, 2010: 134–136). She demonstrates that "repetition is never precise reproduction. One cannot, so to speak, 'say parsley'. And yet in our culture such words can become shibboleths, used to discriminate against those perceived as 'outsiders'" (Perloff 2010: 136; see also Edmond 2019). Some of her works are especially influenced by the visual. For example, her book of bilingual drawings *Plessjør* (2008), her sunrise performance *Raga Down* (2016) and *Together (Doing It)* (2016). In fact, Bergvall insists on the bodily engagement in creation, the engagement of the body, of breathing, of the senses, in making art and literature. The many languages one does not know makes her think of the many ways of communicating one does not know and of the violence of embodied language, for example, in *Cropped*. She is interested in the resonance of spaces, in how sites sing, as in her rewriting of Chaucer's Wife of Bath in *Alisoun Sings* (2019), the final volume of her trilogy that starts with *Meddle English* (2011), followed by *Drift* (2014), her multimedia rewriting of the Old English poem on exile *The Seafarer*. As we read in the Preface to *Alisoun Sings*, Alisoun resonates as a cluster of sounds, as a provocative voice that calls up other voices (Bergvall 2019). Bergvall would probably agree with Merleau-Ponty's concept of "sedimentation of the sensations words procure" (Rabourdin 2020: 2), a process which gives a text its texture, which constructs meaning by the experience we have of words, with all their associations and feelings.

All these are excellent examples that translate words into imagery and into other senses. Experiential translations which border-cross disciplines. Translation processes responding to the whole range of modes inherent in images, words, or sounds, and retranslating with all the translator's senses. Translation Studies now has a heightened interest in the materiality of the new texts and in the performative nature of the semiotic event, including translation itself (Bennett 2019: 2; Littau 2016). Texts are beginning to be conceived dynamically, not as language but as languaging (Baynham and Lee 2019b), which deploys registers, dialects, and other semiotic orders. Thus, the intersemiotic focus "has expanded exponentially due to the work in the visual/gestural/embodied in multimodal communication" and also "translanguaging at the language/body interface, informed by the recent work of Judith Butler (2015)" (Baynham and Lee 2019b: n.p.). Texts are now becoming "a rewriting of a rewriting of a rewriting" in which "translation plays a significant role" (Gentzler 2017: 9–10). Translating thus means considering "the complex movements of texts, not just source to target, but target and beyond, west to east, north to south, linear to non-linear, texts to images, and forward in time and space" (Gentzler 2017: 112–113).

Translation is "a form of writing" and vice versa (Bassnett 2011: 76). Looking is a possible way to deconstruct the power structures that have prevailed and continue to prevail in the (post?) colonial, sexual, economic, or ethnographic eras. That possibility will only be feasible if we look critically. "That means thinking about power relations that produce, are articulated through, and can be challenged by ways of seeing and imaging" (Rose and Tolia-Kelly 2012: 3). The distinction between "vision" and "visuality" is interesting here. More specifically, vision is what the human eye is able to see from a purely physiological point of view, whereas visuality is related to how that vision is constructed, namely, "how we see, how we are able, allowed, or made to see, and how we see this seeing and unseeing therein" (Foster 1998: ix).[13] Conceiving the visual as a field that distills meaning will help us to better understand the very question of meaning. Evidently, this question has no single answer because each new answer depends on the era, context, community, and their way of looking at the world.

Those who have the power to construct "visuality" (Mirzoeff 2006, 2011a, 2011b) have the authority to say what can be seen and how it can be seen. For example, when a crime has been committed, the police order spectators to move away and clear the area. They tell them that there is nothing to see. The right to look is inevitably linked to the ability to face those visual strategies on which power is based. Mirzoeff gives various examples, ranging from the slave plantations and their surveillance devices to the current military-industrial violence performed by drones. Quoting Derrida (1982/1985: xxxvi), he relates the right to look to the invention of the other and to the recognition of otherness. He thus understands "visuality" as the constructed character of vision (see also Mirzoeff 2006; Sturken and Cartwright 2009). Visuality means "how we see how we are able, allowed, or made to see, and how we see this seeing and the unseeing therein" (Foster 1998: ix). As shown in the next chapter, many artists act as translators when they use images to rewrite European cultural values. Bachmann-Medick (2016b: 201–202) gives the following example of an artistranslator:

> the Nigerian English installation artist Yinka Shonibare—his "translation" of a national English painting into a hybrid installation in 1998. In Shonibare's work, Thomas Gainsborough's 1750 painting of an aristocratic couple in the idyllic setting of country life is transformed into a sculpture entitled *Mr. and Mrs. Andrews without Their Heads*. Evoking the guillotine of the French Revolution, the postcolonial artist decapitates the symbolic protagonists of English colonialism, depicting them in African robes displaced from the pastoral context. Through such translation work, Shonibare shows the colonial inscriptions of entangled European/African histories. Here the process of rewriting takes the guise of a redressing and refashioning of European cultural traditions and uses subversive translation strategies to unearth the deep structures of colonial violence.

These are "new translations across fluid borders, entangled modes and senses" (Campbell and Vidal 2019: xl). Other examples are Ghada Amer[14] and her post-translations of characters such as Cinderella, Sleeping Beauty, Snow White, Alice in Wonderland, Tinkerbell, Little Red Riding Hood, or Barbie. They adhere to the death of the author, as announced by Barthes and Foucault in the late sixties, and herald the dissolution of categories such as originality or identity, which are replaced with plagiarism, copy, simulation, de-hierarchy, intertextuality, and entropy. Her "original" works are translations that remind us of Pierre Menard's translation of *Don Quixote* and of Raymond Ferderman's *Surfiction*. They are also reminiscent of Borges, who in *Laberintos* claims that each writer creates his/her own precursor. In all these cases and many others, every writer modifies our conception of the past as the past will modify the future.

In fact, these translations outward are a constant in the art world, a discipline where the meanings of words like "original" and "representation" were understood long before they became part of the translation world. Cases in point include the translation of Goya's *La maja desnuda* (1797) and of Titian's *Venus of Urbino* (1538) by Manet in 1863 with his *Olympia*. Also relevant are the hundreds of rewritings of the *Mona Lisa* by artists such as Corot, Duchamp, or Warhol, as well as those of *Las Meninas*. Some of the countless examples (Bonazzoli and Robecchi 2014) are reminiscent of a painting by David Teniers, which depicts a gallery with many pictures in it.

Translations complete the original, if indeed there is an original. Translations are thoughts about thoughts. Translators look at themselves looking while they inspect a picture of others doing the same. Art and translation unveil how we organize thought. Thought is both situated and constructed. Art reveals that the viewer is

> watching thought. This experience is often self-reflexive. In other words, in addition to viewing the visual organization of the artist's thought, watching thought entails watching one's own thought, exemplified by the visual pattern found in the work of art. Thus, the visual frame-in-the-frame provides viewers with an opportunity to schematise their own thought patterns and their own methods of visual inspection. The frame-in-the-frame in the form of points and lines in the visual field allows us to focus on and begin to define consciousness in its details.
>
> (Minissale 2009: 13)

"A common misconception is that it is the eye that sees . . . Thought has to do with memory and the imagination, logical reasoning, interpretation, and also, emotions. These processes are ways of 'seeing', or rather constructing what is seen" (Minissale 2009: 14).

Vision is a cultural construction. "It is learned and cultivated, not simply given by nature . . . it is deeply involved with human societies, with the ethics and politics. Aesthetics and epistemology of seeing and being seen" (Mitchell 2002: 166). Images "are never transparent windows onto the world" (Rose 2001/2007: 2). They are forms of representation that produce and reproduce social relationships, the genealogy of which needs to be analyzed (Haraway 1991). They are concrete visions of categories such as class, gender, race, or sexuality (Rose 2001/2007: 7).

That is why visuality is linked to power. Mirzoeff advocates a counterhistory of visuality, characterized by a right to look that is relational, egalitarian, and reciprocal. At the same time, he urges us to focus, not so much on the similarities between categories, but rather on their dislocation within the context of the capacities and times that the majority order takes as representative. From this perspective, the encounter with the others "would be the occasion of an archaeology of otherness and dissent, of the common and of the participatory" (Martínez Luna 2012: 26).

In his *Twilight of the Idols*, Nietzsche teaches us that learning to look involves accustoming the eye to gazing calmly and to letting things get closer to the eye. From this perspective, looking means knowing how to contemplate. It is a question of educating the eye and being. Instead of reacting immediately, one must first know when, how, and why to resist, act, and transform.

Looking forces us to finally understand that "the power of images is much greater than generally admitted" (Freedberg 1989: 429). As Barthes (1980/1992) states in his essay on photography, it teaches us that translation depends not on the essence of what is looked at but on the response of s/he who looks, of how we "complete" (Freedberg 1989: 430) what we look at. From this viewpoint, translating becomes an activity that consists of recognizing "the deep cognitive potential that arises from the relations between looking—looking hard—and the figured material object" (*ibid.:* 432).

Nevertheless, taking into account (or not) the multiple interpretations given by Heidegger, Shapiro, or Derrida, among many others, of these pair of worn-out shoes, how do we each reconstruct a painting like Vincent van Gogh's *A Pair of Shoes* (1886)? How do we complete it? How do we translate it? What does it re-present when we look at it? Another example is *Las Meninas*, an absolutely contemporary painting by Diego Velázquez (see Mirzoeff 2016: 31–36), an artist who deeply reflected on the issue of representation and on how to look at our surroundings. *Las Meninas* is a game that projects and reflects the identities of the spectator who looks and the person that is looked at. The painting involves a constant toing and froing until in the end, it is impossible to really know which side of the mirror we are on.

Among other things, *Las Meninas* portrays an image reflected in the back of the space represented. It shows a mirror that reflects King Philip IV of Spain, and his queen. "The intention is to show the painting on which Velázquez is working, in which case it would be the picture of the reflection of a painting" (Hockney and Gayford 2016: 112). The painter is about to begin his work, which is why he is looking so closely at the models. At the same time, he is aware of the subtleties and ambiguities of the situation as a whole. He is standing next to his work, opposite the viewer, whom the painting is destined for. However, the viewer is facing him and thus can only see the back of the canvas. This is the rewriting that the painter will make of a reality, which we in turn are viewing from another perspective. The painting is visible to some but not to others, depending on where the viewer happens to be located. The painter is not only seen in the painting where he is represented, but also in the one where he is representing something. As Foucault (1966) reminds us, he reigns on the threshold of these two incompatible visibilities.

> The formal structure of *Las Meninas* is an encyclopaedic labyrinth of pictorial self-reference, representing the interplay between the beholder, the producer, and the object or model of representation as a complex cycle of exchanges and substitutions . . . it is a *classical* representation of classical representation.
>
> (Mitchell 1994: 58)

What Velázquez proposes in this "meta-metapicture" (Mitchell 1994: 58ff; Mitchell in Grønstad and Vågnes 2017: 183–184) is a game of reverberations, representations and represented. It is a game of appearances, of words and things, and of signifieds and signifiers, which is, in short, the very essence of life.

Looking is a key element in the painting, as analyzed by Michel Foucault in *Les mots et les choses* (1966) and subsequently by Jacques Lacan in seminars 10 and 13 of *The Object of Psychoanalysis* (1966–1967). According to Mitchell, it is a painting "about power and representation", about "the discipline of the eye and control of visual representation", "about the power of painting and the painter, and the power of the sovereign who is the implied observer" (Mitchell 1994: 61). The painter is not so much interested in similarity as in representation, and not so much in the viewers as in his models. Velázquez looks twice at an invisible spectacle, at a space of non-represented invisibility.

As highlighted by Foucault, the painter's eyes seize hold of the spectators, forcing them to enter the picture. The spectators see their invisibility made visible to the painter and transported into an image invisible to themselves. Nobody sees the figures represented in the mirror. Representation is thus unstable. The eye that looks and the eye that is looked at are continuously changing places with each other. The painting is a translation. It is not so much a painting as a game with representation, analogy, and similarities that offers the charm of being halfway between foreground and re-presentation. In fact, it permits us to be seen by the painter, thanks to the same light that allows us to see him. In Velázquez's painting, as in translations, the game of representation not only consists of putting something in the place of something else, but also in unstable superpositions.

A painting, in the same way as a translation, reveals the painter and the translator as much more than the original. This is evident in the many contemporary post-translations of Velazquez's painting, from Picasso to

Manolo Valdés. In *Las Meninas*, as in any translation, the painter/translator looks at us, looks at himself, and paints himself on us. Instead of us entering the painting, it is the painting that overflows onto us (De Diego 2011: 22). Like Velázquez, the translator alters space, a space that with each brushstroke, is fractured through his gaze and ours. We are the readers or spectators, who incorporate into our translation what comes from outside. The important thing is thus not what *is represented* in the painting, but what the painting *represents* (De Diego 2011: 23). As Leo Steinberg (1981: 54) points out, if the painting spoke, it would say, "I see you seeing me—I in you see myself seen—see you seeing yourself being seen—and so on beyond the reaches of grammar".

After the death of Velázquez, the inventory of his belongings revealed that he possessed ten large mirrors, which at that time were very expensive objects. However, other painters were also interested in mirrors. This was the case of Jan van Eyck, who painted a convex mirror in the background of *The Arnolfini Portrait* (1434) (see Hockney and Gayford 2016: 132–135; Han 2011/2017: 54–56 for an analysis) or *Self-portrait in a Convex Mirror* (c. 1524), a painting by the Italian late Renaissance artist Parmigianino, and John Ashbery's 1974 ekphrastic poem about this painting, or Caravaggio's thought-provoking *Narcissus*, an oil painting dating from the end of the sixteenth century. Another interesting artist in this sense is Joshua Reynolds, who in *Self-portrait* (1747–1749) offers a disturbing painting of himself that comes to mind when contemplating Matisse's *The Painter in his Studio* (1916), or Sorolla's *El fotógrafo Christian Franzen* (1903). Reynolds' self-portrait causes uneasiness because the author/painter/translator plays with the viewer. He looks out of the picture as he is being portrayed, related, translated, and at the same time, he translates us. Dazzled by the light, Reynolds is obliged to shade his eyes to peer off into the distance. This creates elusive reflections that fracture the real, and makes us wonder what is he looking at.

Looking inexorably leads us to question the real and the visible because, as John Berger claims in *Ways of Seeing*, the visible does not actually exist. The visible is nothing more than the set of images that the eye creates when looking. Aristotle rightly observed that it is impossible to think without images. However, we should not make the mistake of believing that we can only look with our eyes (Didi-Huberman 1992). Centuries ago, Epicurus insisted that the look is a form of remote touch and that the mythological monster, Medusa, was so hideous that anyone who gazed at her was turned into stone. Perseus was only able to behead her by using a bronze shield as a mirror so that he could see Medusa without directly looking at her.

We look both with our whole body and with language (Didi-Huberman 2008). As observed by Didi-Huberman during the assembly of the exhibition, *Sublevaciones*, we look with words. The real only exists when it is perceived. This depends on how it is perceived, on who looks at it, and on how they see it based on the other. As the author assures us, sight comes before words, and establishes our place in the world. Looking allows us to track the network of relationships behind events (Didi-Huberman 2008: 221). Hans Belting thus constructs his anthropology of images focusing on the bodily interaction with images and the central role "played by an image translation process in which . . . external 'pictures' are transformed into 'mental images' and re-embodied in the individual's visual memory" (Bachmann-Medick 2016b: 253).

Looking means seeing in a certain way, and seeing is also creating (Hudstvedt 2012/2013: 247). This is directly linked to how to translate and how to paint. With each look we take a photograph of the real. We see what we have chosen to see, depending on our *habitus*, to use Pierre Bourdieu's terminology. Indeed, Bourdieu began his analysis of modern societies with studies on photography (Bourdieu 1979b) and museum visits (Bourdieu 1971) to examine the nature of class differences. It is no coincidence that what a social group chooses to photograph symbolically reflects the differences between classes. In other words, the type of image that a group considers important, just like their artistic or gastronomic tastes (Bourdieu 1979a), is directly related to their social class and the inherited or imposed schemes that they use to perceive the real. Every image is, therefore, a way of narrating and translating reality, but above all, it is the result of a way of seeing. That is why ways of seeing reveal ways of understanding the world and are rewritings of the real.

In *Ce que nous voyons, ce qui nous regarde* (1992), Didi-Huberman reminds us of a passage from *Ulysses* at the beginning of Episode 3, "Proteo", where Joyce (1922/1992: 45–46) reflects on the inevitable modality of the visible:

Ineluctable modality of the visible: at least that if no more, thought through my eyes. Signatures of all things I am here to read, seaspawn and seawrack, the nearing tide, that rusty boot. Snotgreen, bluesilver, rust: coloured signs. Limits of the diaphane. But he adds: in bodies. Then he was aware of them bodies before of them coloured. How? By knocking his sconce against them, sure. Go easy. Bald he was and a millionaire, *maestro di color che sanno*. Limit of the diaphane in. Why in? Diaphane, adiaphane. If you can put your five fingers through it, it is a gate, if not a door. Shut your eyes and see.

Stephen closed his eyes to hear his boots crush crackling wrack and shells. You are walking through it howsomever. I am, a stride at a time. A very short space of time through very short times of space. Five, six:

the *nacheinander*. Exactly: and that is the ineluctable modality of the audible. Open your eyes. No. Jesus! If I fell over a cliff that beetles o'er his base, fell through the *nebeneinander* ineluctably. I am getting on nicely in the dark. My ash sword hangs at my side. Tap with it: they do. My two feet in his boots are at the end of his legs, *nebeneinander*. Sounds solid: made by the mallet of *Los Demiurgos*. Am I walking into eternity along Sandymount strand? Crush, crack, crick, crick. Wild sea money. Dominie Deasy kens them a'.

> *Won't you come to Sandymount,*
> *Madeline the mare?*

Rhythm begins, you see. I hear. A catalectic tetrameter of iambs marching. No, agallop: *deline the mare.*

Open your eyes now. I will. One moment. Has all vanished since? If I open and am forever in the black adiaphane. *Basta!* I will see if I can see.

See now. There all the time without you: and ever shall be, world without end.

Joyce encourages us to think through our eyes: "Shut your eyes and see". These are "fragments of listening transformed into fragments of writing" (Voegelin 2018: 9). He constructs with language what the ineluctable modality of the visible imposes on our eyes.[15] And it feeds us with a thought that manifests itself as a physical journey, a journey that passes through the eyes, "thought through my eyes", as the hand passes through a gate. Stephen looks at the outside world, its colors and shapes. However, he also looks at the sounds and touch, the beauty, and ugliness of the real. The changing quality of Proteo guides this episode that evokes the Aristotelian diaphanous, its limits and its denial, the diaphanous and the adiaphan. If you can put your five fingers through, it is a gate, if not, a door.

This is how vision finds touch. Both see and look through language. From their look, bodies impose an ineluctable form of visibility through which we can put our five fingers or not, to finally propose that we close our eyes to see, close our eyes to hear, and listen to a short space of time through very short times of space. It is the ineluctable modality of the audible that allows us to become accustomed to darkness.

> Sound . . . makes the possible thinkable in concrete terms and invites the impossible to reinvigorate an aesthetic and political consciousness and imagination . . . listening to work and to the world to discuss their relationship on a continuum of actuality, possibility and impossibility . . . to write a sounding text, a textual phonography, that does not deny sound

its ephemeral invisibility and mobile intensity . . . but works exactly on the unstable ground and the inexhaustibility of a sonic nature, not to claim comprehension but try curiosity towards the appreciation of awkward and speculative ideas that generate rather than represent thought.

(Voegelin 2018: 5)

The last sentence highlights the importance of generating rather than representing thought through sound in order to keep on moving and creating tensions and dialogues. What we have before us are not only phenotypes but genotexts (Kristeva 1974), because the latter include, in addition to semiotic processes, the advent of symbolic, phonemic resources, such as energy, rhythm, and sound, given that the genotext is not only linguistic but is also a process.

Contrary to phenotype, which besides communicating and denoting, is structured and obeys communication rules, genotext is the result of interrogating language. It is a process in constant motion that moves along the cracks in words. According to Kristeva, semanalysis is based on this distinction between phenotype and genotext. It does not conform to the communicative function of language but rather serves its materiality, insofar as its sounds, rhythms, touch, and smells. Kristeva claims that this concept can be applied to both Mallarme and Joyce. This is also true of *chora*, which is a provisional text type, one in movement that does not depend so much on the real and its representation as on the rhythm that precedes the authenticity, *Chora* is that part of the text that can never be restricted, delimited, or fenced in. It is thus necessary to distinguish between *le sémiotique* and *la sémiotique*, and between conventional semiotics and the symbolic, which includes representations of any kind, including images.

In this context, the dead mother, the one who has definitely closed her eyes to see, allows Stephen to dream the sea in a strange "snotgreen" color. The sea becomes visible and at the same time is mixed with delivery and loss. The bay and the horizon delimit an opaque mass of greenish liquid; and a white porcelain cup contains a thick greenish bile from her rotten liver, rales, and vomiting. These limits of the diaphanous are contained in the bodies. This is Joyce in his purest form, capable of mixing the most beautiful with the most bitter waters and the darkest tides that beat in our eyes and cloud our vision.

Closing the eyes to see means that seeing is not thought and not felt, ultimately, but as an experience of touch (Didi-Huberman 1992). The visible, as Merleau-Ponty pointed out in *Le visible et l'invisible* (1964), is carved in the tangible. Seeing happens in the space of touch. Seeing means touching, and looking implies closing the eyes to see the other better. The eye allows us to see and look and touch sound, which is solid, forged as it is by the mallet of the demiurges. As we walk into eternity along Sandymount Beach, sound looks at us. We have to see if we can see. We have to look if we want to translate.

That is when we realize that nothing simply *is*, but that each single thing represents because each thing looks at us (Didi-Huberman 1992). That is why the conclusion goes beyond closing our eyes to see. The fact is that we open our eyes to experience what we do not see. We look at the world while it looks at us, when we enter and leave it. And we also look at the world when we "show" (in the Wittgenstein sense in *Tractatus*) and finally ask, "how to make this act a shape—a shape that looks at us?" (Didi-Huberman 1992: 18). The answer is far from simple, but it may have to do with the fact that artists and translators produce images. Both create re-presentations of the world and rewrite the real to overcome the Joycean split that occurs with the inescapable modality of the visible.

Notes

1. Different terrors: Georges Didi-Huberman, *Images in Spite of All: Four Photographs from Auschwitz* (Chicago, IL: University of Chicago Press, 2008); W.J.T. Mitchell, *Cloning Terror: The War of Images, 9/11 to the Present* (Chicago, IL: University of Chicago Press, 2011); Susan Sontag, *Regarding the Pain of Others* (New York: Picador, 2004).
2. This gives rise to the interaction between Translation Studies and Imagology, which "does not address the semiotics of cultural difference but focuses on deconstructing ethnotypes and their characterological rationalization of cultural difference" (Flynn *et al.* 2016: 3).
3. For an excellent explanation of the American pictorial turn and the German iconic turn, see Bachmann-Medick 2016b: 245–249.
4. Semiotics in general is very useful for the understanding of new texts, because it considers that a text is a complex. Without going into the different schools of semiotics, what interests us here is the fundamental property of any semiotic system, namely that the sign is in translation a characteristic that ensures that translatability underlies the semantic process. Charles Peirce in particular claims that a sign is not only linguistic but can be any perceptible phenomenon whether related to sight, hearing, smell, or anything else (Gorlée 1997: 311). As already mentioned, Marais (2019: n.p.) has carried out an excellent analysis of Peirce's semiotics as applied to translation. He outlines a theory of translation "which challenges the linguistic bias in translation studies by proposing a semiotic theory that accounts for all the instances of translation, not only interlinguistic translation. In particular, [his work] explores cases of translation which does not include language at all".
5. Eco adds that semiotics is also the discipline that studies everything that can be used to lie, something that could certainly be applied nowadays to the different semiotic systems used in social networks. Some years later, Jonathan Culler (1983) reformulated Eco's definition of sign from the viewpoint of the reader and said that a sign is everything that can be misinterpreted.
6. More information about Sniff Disc is available here: http://translationgames.net/output/p-o-w/

7. This is what some scholars would call "transmediation" (Salmose and Elleström 2020), an intermedia transformation process, where sensorial borders have been crossed. In these cases, the word "translation" is usually avoided to refer to this type of communicative processes because "the word translation provides strong associations with transfers among different verbal languages" (Elleström in Salmose and Elleström 2020: 3; see also Elleström 2021, vol. 1: 75, 83; Elleström 2014: 34). From the "outward turn" and the "translator's gaze" the definition of translation is beginning to expand and these artistic events can be considered examples of translating outward.

8. More information about the project is available here: http://translationgames.net/output/still-in-translation/

9. A virtual version of the exhibition is available here: https://transartation.co.uk

10. For more information: www.bittersuite.org.uk and http://thecuspmagazine.com/uk/tapestries-review/. See also Campbell and Vidal 2019: 335–352.

11. *Eclat* incorporates and reflects on broken English, silence, listening, and intersection between private and public physicality (Bergvall 2000: 15–16). For a reading of "Via" as "an ongoing act", as a performing translation, see Bermann (2014: 286ff).

12. *Flèsh Acoeur* is a graphic tribute piece to Kathy Acker. Bergvall is especially attracted by the novelist's sentence: "I was unspeakable so I ran into the languages of others." Another piece, *Goan Atom* shows a bilingual syntax from both *Flèsh* and the work of Cindy Sherman and Louise Bourgeois.

13. See also Jay's (1993) concept of "ocularcentrism" or Jencks' idea of the centrality of the eye in western culture (1995).

14. Amer's use of translation in many of her pieces has been already analyzed (see for instance Auricchio 2001; Di Paola 2018b).

15. Nicholas Mirzoeff (2011a: xiv) begins one of his most well-known works analyzing this fragment from Joyce's *Ulysses* and concludes that "visuality and its visualizing of history are part of how the West historicizes and distinguishes itself from its others".

3   Translating *With* Art

3.1 Thinking With Art

Contemporary art is no longer a passive object but, as Chambers (2018: v, vi) argues, the active force of a critical disposition: "to transfer the work of art from the stilled status of an object to the active, subjecting force of a critical disposition . . . to think less of art and rather more with art". The whole spirit of art is, according to Robert Barry, "to look ahead to see what's given and to see beyond it. And always question. Never settle for anything. Always question. Always be a threat to the established values—including what you yourself have set up" (Robert Barry in Alberro and Norvell 2001: 98).

Art can alter the ways in which we visualize and conceptualize the world (Holtaway 2021). It is concerned with political violence (Kinna and White-ley 2020). It has been involved in uprisings from the Middle East to Wall Street, in struggles against repressive regimes in Libya and Egypt, and in issues such as climate change, gender violence, and racism (Serafini 2018). In this context, the contemporary work of art is understood as a way of see-ing. Without explicit recourse to the "outward turn in translation", the art world has been rewriting the Real and playing with the concept of repetition and re-presentation for decades. As Adorno (1970/2002: 124) noted forty years ago, "in recent aesthetic debates, especially in the fine arts, the con-cept of *écriture* has become relevant . . . all artworks are writing".

As Campbell and Vidal (2019: xxv) claim when referring to intersemi-otic translation, this chapter argues that art goes on "a journey alongside or across borders which are not always obvious". Art communicates and translates reality "on many levels" (*id.*). From this perspective, art

> leaves the shores of representation—the "mimesis" of some "thing" that "authentically" grounds the work—to propose an ethical event . . . the work itself is not merely an addition to the existing canon . . . but

becomes a critical interrogation and potential interruption that recon-
figures its terms, reworks its tempos and reroutes its premises.

(Chambers 2018: v)

In this light, contemporary artwork offers different ways of seeing. It
opens (our) space to unfamiliar accents, which are close to others who may
reject our transformation of their languages. Art transports art elsewhere,
and therefore translates us:

> For what is rendered explicit in translation is not merely the contin-
> gency of language and our movement in its midst, but also the per-
> sistent interrogation seeded by ambiguity, uncertainty, reformulations,
> semantic shifts and contestation. . . . The provocative and productive
> force of translation, as a continual negotiation of being in the world,
> can be traced in multiple forms and formations: in the phenomenology
> of everyday life, in musical, pictorial and literary aesthetics, in clothing
> and culinary practices.
>
> (Chambers 2018: 33–34)

Throughout history, the artist's gaze has translated the world from different points of view—sometimes offering the perspective of the patron, and at
others, especially in the contemporary era, translating with various semiotic
systems the look of the most vulnerable. The look that translates should do
so from a position of respect, a word that literally means "to look back",
and also approach the other without the presumption of understanding him/
her/it completely:

> Literally, *respect* means "to look back." It stands for consideration and
> caution [*Rücksicht*]. Respectful interaction with others involves refrain-
> ing from curious *staring*. Respect presupposes a distanced look—the
> *pathos of distance*. Today, it is yielding to the obtrusive staring of
> *spectacle*. The Latin verb *spectare*, from which *spectacle* derives, is
> voyeuristic gazing that lacks deferential consideration—that is, respect
> (*respectare*). Distance is what makes *respectare* different from *spec-
> tare*. A society without respect, without the pathos of distance, paves
> the way for the society of scandal.
>
> (Han 2013/2017: 1)

Richard Sennett (2003: 183) accurately defines respect not simply as an
action but as an attitude that

> also requires a relationship in which one party accepts that it cannot
> understand something of the other. The acceptance that there are things

of the other that one cannot understand gives both permanence and equality to the relationship. Autonomy implies connection and at the same time otherness.

Translating from respect means looking again. Looking at the other from the *pathos* of distance, not as a spectacle. Distinguishing *respectare* from *spectare* is the key. Looking to translate, translate as a way of looking, is to become closer to the other, to know that the other also looks at us, and that that look counts. Digital media, liquid society, transparent society, and weak thinking causes the disappearance of the real. The smartphone erases all negativity and

> acts as a digital mirror for the new post-childhood edition of the mirror stage. It opens a narcissistic state, a sphere of the imaginary, in which I include myself. The other does not speak through the smartphone. . . . The look is the other in the image, which looks at me and fascinates me. It is the punctum, which rips the homogeneous fabric of the studium. As the gaze of the other it is opposite the eye, which delights in the image. It pierces the charm of the eyes and questions my freedom. The growing narcissism of perception makes the look disappear, makes the other disappear.
>
> (Han 2013/2017: 44, 45)

Marcel Duchamp's *étant donnés*, *Merda de artista* by Piero Manzoni, *Red Flow* by Judy Chicago, the folded blankets of Barry Flanagan, the vacuum cleaners of Jeff Koons, the *Brillo Box* by Andy Warhol, the *Anthropometries of the Blue Period* by Yves Klein, the Fluxus *performances*, or the museum of modern art by Marcel Broodthaers are imagetexts, rewritings, and post-translations, which look at the world in a different way and demand a different look of the viewer. In these and many other cases, the work of art offers a new reading of an ordinary object, as Marjorie Perloff (in Andersson 2018: 34) claims with reference to Duchamp's *In Advance of the Broken Arm*: "craft is replaced by choice . . . [Duchamp] took an ordinary article of life, placed it so that its useful significance disappeared under the new title and point of view". These rewritings exemplify translation "as a revolutionary act, in that it brings ideas and forms across cultural boundaries, offering life-changing possibilities" (Gentzler 2017: ix).

The world that they look at and which is looked at is not that of the Quattrocento oil painting. On the contrary, it is another, fragmented, hybrid world, which was initially revealed in the kaleidoscopic seeing of the *collage* artists and in the brittle planes of expressionists. It was also present in geometric abstraction, which forced viewers to think about a crisis of representation and the urgency of looking at other worlds and from other worlds, starting, this time, from points, colors, or lines on a plane (Klee, Miró, Kandinsky) or geometries (Mondrian, Malevitch, Lissitzky).

Art teaches us what reality that is not reality is like. It also shows us what this reality would be if we decided to look at it in another way. Works like these and others are examples of the "outward turn in translation studies" since they translate with semiotic systems other than words. From the perspective of the outward turn, these artists are "agent[s] of the transformation of a text" (Bassnett 2014b: 169), who show that translations today are "a constant and dynamic flow of changing versions" (Bassnett 2014b: 176).

They are post-translations because they have eliminated the limits of purely linguistic communication and do not understand translation as a product or a short-term process but rather as "[a] cultural condition underlying communication" (Gentzler 2017: 7). They are works that reinterpret the Real, based on the cultural context in which they are inserted. They are thus post-translated for a new audience, avoiding any border or boundary between disciplines. They translate reality with forms, colors, images, and languages that are "not confined to linguistic borders" and which open up "a myriad of possibilities to carry form and sense from one culture into another beyond the limitations of words. At the same time, such processes impact on the source artefact enriching it with new layers of understanding" (Campbell and Vidal 2019: xxvi).

This chapter underlines the presence of a wide range of different art media, from painting and photography to media artwork and net art. These media translate by using different languages as a material through a variety of perceptual channels, which transform language into a spatial, aural, and visual experience (Benthien *et al.* 2019). The artists mentioned in what follows play with words, colors, bodies, sounds, and movement. They appropriate material from literary texts, create narratives, use voice-overs, and arguably adopt similar strategies to those employed by translators, in order to show different ways of perceiving the world. In their image and multimedia installations, video performances, digital video art and net art are based on web technologies that are not present in institutional contexts and can only be accessed online. They use acts of translation as their starting point to rewrite identities, margins, borders, and migrations, and in sum to address issues such as the crossing of cultures, globalization, or hybridization that are common concerns to both disciplines.

3.2 Words in Art

The Renaissance was a period that developed a particular modality of representation. Man (not woman) became the measure of the universe and Europe was the measure of everything. It also inaugurated the modern worldview and "the mechanisms that translated the planet into a world picture" (Chambers 2017: 17). The oil painting era (1500–1900), with its linear or one-point perspective, was followed by the avant-garde period. This was the time of Cézanne in his paintings and writings but also the Cubists and Futurists with their "image montages, collages of linguistic and visual materials, or the integration of ready-mades and found footage" (Benthien *et al.* 2019: 2). These artists were the precursors of language-based media art and net art.

The Surrealists, the Dadaists and their "Bruitist poem", "simultaneous poem", and "movement poem", the Abstract Expressionists and other movements, introduced and deconstructed the topic of similarity. The principle of perspective is thus subverted. This evidently has important consequences because it means deconstructing the old concept of the unique representation of things. Accordingly, art begins to offer different translations of reality. The adoption of multiple points of view, thanks to the deconstruction of the figure in a cubist painting, is a statement that point of view or any hegemonic point of view, has disappeared. Examples include the Suprematist painting, *Red Square and Black Square*, by Malevitch (1915, New York, MOMA) and *Composition* by Mondrian (1916, New York, Guggenheim).

Words play an important role in the work of many artists (Jaworski 2014). Marcel Duchamp and Salvador Dalí created works which are "a linguistic investigation of the image" (London in Campbell and Vidal 2019: 133). René Magritte is one of the best-known artists who uses images and texts in his canvases. In many of his paintings, he *writes* about the gap between the seeable and the sayable, such as in *La clef des songes* (1935). That is the gap that must be translated, because it is where the relation between language as a communication system and its adaptation to the empirical world is born.

Ceci n'est pas une pipe (1928) is a "metapicture" (Mitchell 1994: 64–74) where Magritte shows the incision of discourse in the shape of things. We inevitably relate the text to the drawing, but at the same time, there is a contradiction between the word and the painted object (Broodthaers 1988: 39). There is nothing in the word "pipe" similar to a pipe, nor, as William James once pointed out, does the word "dog" bite. Magritte criticizes the tyranny of words and like Wittgenstein, sometimes names things that are not necessary to name (Gablik 1976: 126). Magritte dodges the affirmative discourse on which similarity is based and puts in check the hope of pure similitude in favor of the instability of a space without reference points (Foucault 1973/1983). Magritte is the best of translators since his rewritings of reality dissociate the similitude of similarity. He claims that painting (like translating) is not a question of stating, but rather of tying verbal signs and plastic elements to each other through layers and layers of layers. This avoids the background of affirmative discourse on which similarity rests and puts into play pure unstable similitudes (Foucault 1973/1983). The pipe is thus not a pipe because it is the representation of a pipe.

Magritte's logoiconic paintings include the non-pipe series (*L'Aube à l'Antipode, La Trahison des Images,* and others). In his *Ecrits*, he asks, "Who could smoke the pipe of one of my paintings? No one. Therefore, IT IS NOT A PIPE." *Madame Recamier* (1949) and *L'Art de la conversation* (1950) address the autonomous gravitation of things that form their own words. *La trahison des images* represents "the relation between discourse and representation . . . the gap between words and pictures" (Mitchell 1994: 65). All of them and many others, for instance *Les liaisons dangereuses* (1935), deal with "the old space of representation" (Foucault 1973/1983: 41; see also Mitchell 1994: 67–74).

The painter thus questions the relationship between words and things, and between things and their representation. His translation of the "real" pipe is his way of looking and seeing the pipe. Another painter or translator would have rewritten it, re-represented it, from another viewpoint or perspective. S/he would have made another translation of the pipe. In fact, Magritte translates his translation of the pipe in *Les deux mystères* (1966). *Le miroir faux* (1928), *Le plagiat* (1940), and *La leçon d'anatomie* (1943) show the experience of the double. *Le balcon* (1950) translates or rewrites from Goya and Manet.

Magritte's "real aim is to show what cannot be pictured or made readable, the fissure in representation itself, the bands, the layers, and fault-lines of discourse, the blank space between the text and the image" (Mitchell 1994: 69). Magritte's paintings, such as *La page blanche* (1967), are looks that look and look at us, so that in turn, we look at a way among many others of facing or translating reality. They are a constant reminder that no translation, not even the first or "original", is unique, definitive, and motionless. As Foucault argues in his ekphrasis of *Las Meninas*, we cannot ever say what we see, given that what we see never resides in what we say. Magritte rewrites a pipe which is his pipe. He does not use words to translate how he views the pipe.

> The translator effectively plays the role of mediator in an experiential process that allows the recipients (viewer, listener, reader or participant) to re-create the sense (or "semios") of the source artefact for themselves (Campbell 2017: 179–180). This holistic approach recognizes that there are multiple possible versions of both source and target texts and this can help mitigate the biases and preconceptions a static, intralingual translation can sometimes introduce.
>
> (Campbell and Vidal 2019: xxvi)

Translating means rewriting Foucault's *écart*, that infinite relation, scission, and point of difference between seeing and saying (Foucault 1966: 26). Translation is a Derridean polylogue that avoids a master voice by asking, as Lyotard (1987), did, about the possibility of speaking the visual and of visualizing language.[1] Language is used in contemporary art as an image to translate the Real. In 1969, Joseph Kosuth (1991) published his essay, "Art After Philosophy", which laid the foundations of conceptual art. He uses words as art:

> Joseph Kosuth's *Art as Idea as Idea (Art)*, 1967, is a photograph (48 × 48 in) mounted on board. The artwork is visible and yet, if understood as a gallery label or dictionary entry, it is referring to art as an absent, invisible or abstract concept. It piques interest by inviting a perceptual examination of the shapes of the letters as 'art', yet also invites us to override this response, encouraging us to reflect on the nature of vision and art. There are many works of art that use puns and word games to present the viewer with visual paradoxes. . . . In Kosuth's image, we alternate reading a text with seeing an image. . . . The artwork adopts a mutually reinforcing strategy: it suggests a reading between the lines and its visual equivalent, an understanding beyond optical sensation. . . . In Kosuth's work, which relies heavily on words and images, reading becomes the subject of visual art.
>
> (Minissale 2013: 119)

In 1965 Kosuth exhibited *One and Three Chairs* (the same idea was developed with *One and Three Lamps* and other objects). This work explores the linguistic nature of art and the interactions between semiotic manifestations. Kosuth places a chair in front of a viewer, the photo of that same chair, and the dictionary definition of the word "chair". In this way, he poses the problem of representation by focusing on the fact that the relationship between words and things is manifested in signs. He is also saying that signs are very different and can manipulate reality. Without a doubt, this work is one of the best possible definitions of how to translate outward, since it rewrites the chair with different semiotic systems, beyond boundaries between disciplines, a "radical review" (Gentzler 2015: 2) of what translation is. It exemplifies what was mentioned in the first chapter, that translation focuses "on broader translinguistic aspects and transcultural processes" (Bassnett 2011: 72). Another artist, another translator, would have chosen another type of chair, and that chair would have translated the Real in another way and from another ideology (in André Lefevere's conception of ideology).

In addition, Kosuth's photograph of that chair is a translation of it. It is Berger's way of seeing the chair, based on a non-linguistic semiotic code.

Again, another photographer could present, re-present, see, and look at that chair in a different way. Finally, Kosuth's third translation or third way of seeing the chair is its dictionary definition. All dictionaries define things with words chosen in consonance with the historical moment or cultural context. This is the case of the definition of words loaded with emotional and political connotations in countries governed by dictatorial regimes.

Each person experiences differently the representation that words create of an object, entity, color, or sound; and each person translates each image or form differently. *Five Works in Orange Neon* is from that same year (1965), another of the many works in which the artist uses neon lights and language. This time he draws his inspiration from the concept of tautology as developed by Ludwig Wittgenstein. Something similar happens with *Three Adjectives Described* (1965), *Clock (One and Five)* (1965), *One Color, Five Adjectives* (1966) and *Four Colors Four Words* (1966). However, Kosuth's pictorial work is not his only example of outward translation. The same thing occurs with *Purloined* (2000), a novel "composed entirely of single pages from more than a hundred different novels of various genres to form a single work. Each page is photocopied directly from its original source, thus resulting in a variety of typefaces and layouts" (Dworkin and Goldsmith 2011: 331).

Conceptual artists—Kosuth but also many others, such as Sol LeWitt (with his "structures" and "wall drawings"), Ed Ruscha's intersections of photography, text and painting, Dan Flavin (who makes art with light), and Joan Brossa's visual poems to mention only a few[2]—juxtapose images and texts. They use words as their primary medium in the form of proposition, where language is used materially (Kalyva 2016; Andersson 2018). However, what they create is secondary to how it is created (Goldsmith 2011: 125ff). That is why Kosuth argues that in this context, a work of art is a translation, a kind of proposition which is not factual but linguistic in nature. In other words, it does not describe the behavior of physical or even mental objects. It expresses the formal consequences of the definitions of art (Kosuth 1991).

Some artwork consists of imagetexts, as Mitchell would call them. They confirm that there will always be a gap between words and looks, between the original and its translation, between the gaze that looks and the one that looks at us. The fact that many artists use words in their canvases does not mean that the use of words in art is directly linked to the idea of translation. However, it does show the capacity of art to deconstruct boundaries between disciplines. "Experiments with letters, words, and literary structures indicate that language and literature are at least as important for contemporary audiovisual arts as they were for the avant-garde visual arts" (Benthien *et al.* 2019: 2). For instance, in the early seventies, Lawrence

Weiner produced works consisting of words painted on the walls of a gallery. Each phrase is a work of art where the binarism, original/reproduction, is undermined:

> People, buying my stuff, can take it wherever they go and can rebuild it if they choose. If they keep it in their heads, that's fine too. They don't have to buy it to have it—they can have it just by knowing it. Anyone making a reproduction of my art is making art just as valid as art as if I had made it.
>
> (Weiner 1972: 217)

Decades later, in another interview, Weiner again comments on the idea of reproduction. Today's "post-translation" is based on a very similar idea of "originals":

> basic to my aesthetic is that the reproduction of a piece of mine is as equally valid as art, as the "original." Whereas the wall removal I did in Bern, the *36_ _ 36_ Removal of Plaster Lathing from a Wall* . . . That piece, if somebody walked in and saw it, and got excited by it and went home and did it on their wall, in the physical sense, that piece is just as much art. And it is my art. But it is a reproduction of my art. And it's just as valid aesthetically as the one that was in the museum or the one that was in the gallery or somewhere else.
>
> (Weiner in Alberro and Norvell 2001: 102)

And he comments on language and translation in his art:

> I like language very much because it's ambiguous. The ambiguity of language attracts me much more. Say a photograph is static, and any time there is a photo, it's always accompanied with language. When you read the language, or when you translate the language from one language to another language to another language, which is part of the new work I've been doing, you add to the ambiguity of the piece.
>
> (*ibid.*: 107)

Weiner is not focused on what words mean or on the fact that they are words. His interest lies in reading words for their meaning and the fact that they will place that meaning within the sculptural context of their parameters. The texts inserted in his works are "always sculptures . . . so what everybody calls texts and sentences . . . are functioning as art" (Weiner in Buchloh 1998/2017: n.p.).

Another example of many is Robert Barry, who does not feel comforta-
ble with the label "conceptual artist". He uses color to contextualize words.
Each word is carefully selected and treated as an image whose position,
size, length, color, and so on, confers meaning. He also works with translators when his works are exhibited outside the United States. Collaborating
with his translators, he realizes that words have nuances as well as different possibilities. He seems to be open to different and more interesting
meanings:

> Lately, I've been working in French, and German, and Dutch, and hav-
> ing an interesting time working with translations. I mean, in your own
> mind the words are always translated into what you want them to mean
> anyway. . . . I have to work with a translator who becomes a collabora-
> tor. Sometimes it takes more than one translator to get some idea of
> the possible meanings that might be usable. I present a list of words
> that I think might be appropriate and then what I get back are either
> statements saying that a word is untranslatable or has no single equiva-
> lent. Or they come up with three or four other possibilities and we get
> together and discuss them. Sometimes the ideas submitted are much
> more interesting than what I originally had in mind. . . . This idea of
> working in other languages—an installation in Germany went through
> about four or five different translations, including those of the student
> helpers who questioned the meanings even as they were painting the
> words onto the wall. So, even then, it was getting a final interpretation
> of my original ideas. I found that wonderful, absolutely. As soon as it
> was translated, it got out my control a little bit. It opened up a whole
> other more flexible area.
>
> (Barry in Welish *et al*. 1994: 39)

Artists use words as images in their verbal art to demonstrate how concepts may travel between semiotic systems and how those concepts can be
translated in different ways through different media. These artists "translate
across" genres and disciplines. They are concerned "with the marginal, the
gaps, fissures and contradictions of working in the interstices between these
various boundaries" (Bal and Morra 2007: 7). This is how translation can
learn from art. These works are Barthesian "texts". Accordingly, they can
be perceived as tissues of citations resulting from the thousand sources of
culture. These artistic ways of seeing show how to translate with images and
how in these rewritings, translation is not "merely a footnote in history, but
one of the most important vital forces available to introduce new ways of
thinking and introducing significant cultural change" (Gentzler 2017: 3).[3]

3.3 Art That Post-translates: Cindy Sherman

A highly relevant example of translation outward, where an artist rewrites by leaping into other territories, is that of Cindy Sherman. She post-translates, translates outward by using her own body[4] as a text that rewrites other bodies in order to deconstruct the male gaze (Mulvey 1991; Solomon-Godeau 1991a; Jones 1997; Silverman 1996; Ch'i Liu 2010; Bronfen 2018). Her work has been analyzed as a clear example of postmodern American art and as art that foregrounds the politics of representation (Crimp 1979; Danto 1990; Solomon-Godeau 1991b; Owens 1992). Also as "key for the study of visual culture" (Mirzoeff 2016: 51).

By rewriting Berger's (1972: 47) well-known assertion, "Men look at women. Women watch themselves being looked at", she exemplifies Campbell and Vidal's (2019: xxix) "translator's gaze", "the intense engagement of the translator with the source text which also entails an appropriation of sorts—not just with the eyes but with all other senses". Sherman translates *sans borders*, she translates with the body and turns translation into an experiential process, as in Campbell and Vidal's approach.[5] Her translations show how many different kinds of text contain translational elements that are rarely considered.

> To conduct such an analysis, translation studies scholars of necessity need to bring in academics from other disciplines such as politics, sociology, anthropology, and psychology; from linguistics and literary studies, cultural studies, gender, race, and class studies, to be able to see and measure the translational effects. Indeed, nearly every discipline derives from and depends upon translation, a dependency that will only increase in the future. Contemporary and increasingly interdisciplinary studies of translation suggest that borders transgressed in translation tend to be more multiple and permeable than traditionally conceived.
>
> (Gentzler 2017: 5)

By photographing herself, she rewrites the most stereotyped roles of contemporary women (housewife, secretary, prostitute, etc.). She translates what is already a reproduction. Sherman's self-translations are also our self-translations: she makes us aware

> of the constructed nature of the camera's gaze and the power that is inherent in that gaze. . . . Sherman's mirror is a distorting, cracked glass, which does not permit us to see her but to see ourselves looking at her.
>
> (Mirzoeff 1995: 131)

She rewrites those stereotypes created by a patriarchal society for women:

> the fiction Sherman discloses is the fiction of the self. Her photographs show that the supposed autonomous and unitary self out of which those other "directors" would create their fictions is itself nothing other than a discontinuous series of representations, copies, fakes. Sherman's photographs are all self-portraits in which she appears in disguise enacting a drama whose particulars are withheld. This ambiguity of narrative parallels the ambiguity of the self that is both actor in the narrative and creator of it. For though Sherman is literally self-created in these works, she is created in the image of already-known feminine stereotypes; her self is therefore understood as contingent upon the possibilities provided by the culture in which Sherman participates, not by some inner impulse. As such, her photographs reverse the terms of art and autobiography. They use art not to reveal the artist's true self, but to show the self as an imaginary construct. There is no real Cindy Sherman in these photographs; there are only the guises she assumes. And she does not create these guises; she simply chooses them in the way that any of us do. The pose of authorship is dispensed with not only through the mechanical means of making the image, but through the effacement of any continuous, essential persona or even recognizable visage in the scenes depicted.
>
> (Crimp 1980: 99)

Sherman's works are self-portraits of an identity that is masked, an identity in disguise. She post-translates through her own body, through new ways of seeing. Her translated identities

> glance anxiously outside the frame of some unspecified menace, thereby implying the presence of a narrative even while withholding it. This "still effect" . . . compels a typological reading: Sherman's women are not women but images of women, specular models of femininity projected by the media to encourage imitation, identification; they are, in other words, tropes, figures.
>
> (Owens 1992: 84)

In the light of the translation turn, it can be said that Sherman's women are not women but translations of women. She uses photography but "doesn't consider herself a photographer. . . . 'The only reason I don't call myself a photographer is that I don't think other people who consider themselves photographers would think I'm one of them'" (Morris 1999: 12). Her images are signs shaking imposed signs, rewritings that aim to challenge and to fissure the stereotyped representation of meaning. Sherman has a particular view of translation:

> Translation is not seen as a form of importing a text from the outside, but rather drawing upon reserves and experiences from within each individual and one's own multicultural heritage. In this context, translation is not a mechanical activity applied to a text, but the very living substance of both the source and target text, a living, malleable, formable matter.
>
> (Gentzler 2015: np)

Sherman shows women's bodies as texts translated by different cultures which construct them not as realities but as products of ideology and symbolic violence. In many of her photographs (i.e., *Untitled 96*, the world's most expensive photograph sold at Christie's in 2011 for 3.9 million dollars), Sherman looks at women meant to interest the male gaze. Decades before the outward turn and post-translation, she seems to answer Gentzler's (2017: 5) question, "what if we erase the border completely and rethink translation as an always ongoing process of *every* communication?".

In our contemporary culture, there is a demand for "a questioning of older definitions of translation, and an end to trying to distinguish between so-called originals, translations, and rewritings" (Bassnett in Gentzler 2017: ix). For instance, in the 1980s she rewrites the Brothers Grimm in her surreal and horrific pictures based on fairy tales. Her *Untitled Film Stills* re-translate those stereotypes that patriarchal society have imposed on women. Her photographs can even be conceived as four layered translations:

> Sherman's "poses" have at least four levels of presentation: Cindy Sherman as Sherman; Sherman playing an unknown woman; Sherman playing an unknown woman playing an actress; Sherman playing an unknown woman playing an actress through the eyes of the male gaze. . . . Sherman destabilizes any phenomenological approach to images because we can never be sure what is being represented and what is being experienced . . . her work is worrying because it suggests that any such facticity is always presented, or self-presented, and through a tissue of lies, through layers of fantasy, veils of social power and desire, and through the interpolation of mass media semiotics.
>
> (Minissale 2013: 209, 210)

Furthermore, *Untitled 96* was subsequently post-translated by Yasumasa Morimura, whose gaze subverts even the most transgressive paintings, as is the case of this disturbing post-translation. Morimura is a contemporary translator who demonstrates that art situates the look. In his *Criticism and the Lover A*, he translates Cézanne's *Apples and Oranges*. Again, he rewrites Manet in his 1989 painting, *Daughter of Art History Theatre*. Morimura's look is a sinister post-translation of what was once a new translation of reality. As he does with Frida Kahlo, Duchamp, Cézanne, and Manet, among others, Morimura creatively translates Sherman's *Untitled #96*:

> in such a way as to suggest continual transpositions of self. Morimura performs the role of a woman playing a film role, playing Cindy Sherman, playing a woman, playing a film role. These various "masks" fit perfectly into the postmodernist theory of the self and simulacra: not only is the self elusive, it is also plural and yet "appropriative" of previous selves and fictional roles. Role playing and public personas become part of a process of self-referencing, using multiple indexes (woman, transvestite man, film star, artist, performer) any or all of which can be combined. In processing these personae imaginatively, the viewer also acquires a sense of flux because her reality testing, by which a moment can be fixed as real in order to reflect on what one is looking at, is as elusive as the identity depicted.
>
> (Minissale 2013: 231–232).

These works remind us that the translator is that self who deconstructs heterogeneous but also stereotyped territories. Cindy Sherman is the post-translator of reality who looks and is looked at, who photographs herself adopting a thousand and one identities, protecting and unprotecting herself with a thousand and one masks. In the translator, as in the Sherman artist, several selves coexist, as in the author of the original text. Sherman, and Sherman the artist, who is a concatenation of stereotypes, reproduces what is already a reproduction and becomes someone who looks but who is also an object of desire, an object of looks that are sometimes obscene, sometimes dominant, but always from the panoptic. Translations that look at the world and when they look, see entire worlds, reveal to us that texts are made of splinters that cannot be removed without pain. Like Sherman's gaze, the translator's gaze is constantly redefining new egos or dissolving in them.

Sherman's *History Portraits* (1991) is another excellent example of how artists translate past images with new ones. Arcimboldo, Raphael, Dürer, Rubens, Caravaggio, Boucher, Ingres, and Picasso, are thus rewritten through color, form, image, bodies (Döttinger 1995/2012; Danto 1991). Her *History Portraits* demonstrate Gentzler's (2017: 10) already mentioned claim, apropos of Sherry Levine, that "all writing is rewriting . . . a rewriting of a rewriting of a rewriting". Sherman's photographs/translations act as mask-mirrors that give back to the reader the responsibility of the panoptic to look without being seen. Being visible without seeing alienates. Seeing without being seen gives power. The encounter between our gaze and that of the reader may give rise to the monotony of a monochorde gaze, which deep down is nothing but one of the Foucaultian disciplinary techniques. It is that look that transforms the other into an object or stereotype condemned by Laura Mulvey (1975). On the contrary, this crossing of looks could also result in the counterpoint of voices as described by Said (1993).

Sherman creates layers and layers of layers. With her palimpsests she calls into question the uniqueness of the original, and the originality of the author. Thus, in his *Theory*, Kenneth Goldsmith (2015: n.p.) claims the following:

> If you are not making art with the intention of having it copied, you're not really making art for the 21st-century.
>
> Authenticity is another form of artifice.
>
> Start copying what you love. Copying, copying, copying. At the end of the copy, you will find yourself.
>
> We don't need the new sentence. The old sentence reframed is good enough.
>
> There are no "correct" readings. Only reproductions and possibilities.
>
> I copy pre-existing texts and move information from one place to another.

By translating outward, artists like Sherman show to what extent these two terms—originality and repetition—are bound together in a kind of aesthetic economy, interdependent and mutually sustaining, though originality has long been the most highly valued term whereas repetition, copy, reduplication, translation were discredited. These translations reinforce the discredited half of the pair, the one that opposes the multiple to the singular, the reproducible to the unique, and the fraudulent to the authentic (Krauss 1986: 9–12).

3.4 Translation in Contemporary Art

Although they may seem to be separate disciplines, all these artists and many others are examples of transdisciplinary encounters between contemporary art and translation. Although it is still an under-explored area in Translation Studies, research in the art world has already focused on translation and some journals have contributed to this encounter between contemporary art and translation. Thus we have *Journal of Visual Art, Word & Image* and *Art in Translation*. International conferences have also been held, for instance *Art in Translation: International Conference on Language and the*

Arts (Reykjavik 2012) and *Art i Traducció* (Vic, 5 November 2019). We saw in the previous chapters examples of architects who consider buildings as spatial texts, dancers who translate previously told stories through their bodies in movement, artists who rewrite poems through scent and other senses. Joanna Morra (2000: 129, 132), Founding Principal Editor of *Journal of Visual Art*, understands art history "as a translative practice . . . writing art history is a mode of translation". Important contributions have also been made by Jacques Derrida, Jean François Lyotard, Douglas R. Hofstadter, William J.T. Mitchell, Mieke Bal, Édouard Glissant, Emily Apter, Paola Zaccaria, Jacques Lezra, and Gary Shapiro, who echo this heterotopia and transversality among the arts. There are relevant publications which very recently keep highlighting these transdisciplinary encounters between contemporary art and translation—for example, it is significant that The Whitechapel Gallery published a reader in 2019 (The Documents of Contemporary Art series) that "seeks to assert the role of contemporary art in cultural translation" (Williamson 2019: 14) and that sees translation "as much more than transferring one language to another, but its ability to communicate and enable individuals to be *heard*" (*id.*).[6]

In addition, the art world has not only seen this need to address translation from the viewpoint of theory but also from practice. Translation Studies has still not sufficiently focused on this point. Exceptions include the PhD theses of Modesta Di Paola (2015) and Anna Dot (2019), which offer excellent examples of artists who reflect on the concept of translation. A good example is Antoni Muntadas and his project, *On Translation* (Apter 2006: 204–206, 2013: 106–107, 2014; Vidal in press), a series starting in 1995 which today includes 69 works and is still ongoing. Muntadas is interested in translation in spaces of fear and conflict, such as borders. He highlights the importance of language(s), accents, and (in)communication. His art projects are translations of contemporary asymmetrical spaces. For Muntadas, translation is cultural rewriting. His projects show that the South translates fear of the Other in a different way from the North:

> From 2003 to 2005 I was working in Tijuana and San Diego on a project I titled *On Translation: Fear/Miedo*. The work process made me think of the similarities with the area between southern Spain and northern Africa, for the latter represents "the door" to Europe just as the former represents "the door" to the USA. While obtaining information and compiling data in the region of the Strait from the beginning of 2006 I have perceived a number of similarities but also great differences. Similarities in displacements, crossings, survival, the search for a better life, the idealization of consumption, of the construction of what is often a media reality. Differences due, on the one hand, to the

added complexity of religion and its influences, and on the other, to the problems caused by terrorism . . . *On Translation: Miedo/Jauf* is not a work on African/European emigration/immigration. Nor is it a work on religion or on terrorism. Two different realities separated not by the sea but by border fences and boundaries on both sides. The search for the North, with its man-made paradises that for many remain lost; fear as an emotion/sensation inserted in the decision of crossing. The construction of the South as a fiction/reality linked to the phenomena of the unknown, exoticism and difference. The attraction (and rejection) of two different realities in which information circulates from person to person via the media and through stereotypes.

(Muntadas 2008: 214)

Muntadas' projects eloquently show how the art world explicitly uses translation. This is also reflected in *A Case Study for Transference* (1994), by the Chinese artist Xu Bing,[7] whose pieces act as intercultural mediations that address the relationship between East and West. Other examples include the legibility and translatability of calligraphy, as in the work of Zhang Huan and of (un)translatability, in Wenda Gu's work entitled *Forest of Stone Steles: Retranslation & Rewriting of Tang Dynasty Poetry* (1993–2005).

Likewise, there is art that raises the question of translation between artistic languages and languages along with the ensuing cultural, social, and political consequences, as reflected in the work of Chantal Ackerman, Ghada Amer, Andrea Frank, and others. There is also translation between very diverse media (e.g., writing, sculpture, video, performance, dance, cinema, and theatre). A case in point is the work of Joan Jonas, some of whose performances are translations of Borges's labyrinths and mirrors to another medium (e.g., *Mirror Pieces*, 1969). There is also the poem, *The Wind Sleepers*, by HD in the performance *I Want to Live in the Country (And Other Romances)* (1976), or *Helen in Egypt* and *Tribute to Freud*, both by Hilda Doolittle. In *Lines in the Sand* (2002), she post-translates the story of Helen of Troy to the Luxor Hotel casino in Las Vegas, as well as President Bush's first statements to Saddam Hussein at the beginning of the Gulf War.

Still another example is Shirin Neshat, an artist straddling two worlds (Iran and the United States) and two languages (Persian and English). Using photography, video, and cinema, she creates visual poems that capture the situation of women in Iran and show completely opposite ways of thinking. She mixes images and words (in fact, her works cannot be exhibited in Iran because of the texts in Arabic that she superimposes on bodies). Her fluid visual texts disregard boundaries and never offer a single meaning or provide an answer. For her, language is a means of asserting cultural identity.

As a result, Farsi calligraphy on female hands and faces is a way for women to show how they are forced into submission and silence.

In a recent interview, Shirin Neshat argues that the inscription of texts over specific parts of the female body are very significant. "In Islamic culture, the majority of the body is covered with the veil. In my photographic work and in the video, I really focus on the parts of the body that are allowed to be revealed, like the face, the hands, the feet. They are able to say a lot by simply presenting the palm of their hands. These hands raised are kind of a symbol of protest".[8] Neshat post-translates between disciplines, as in her film, *Women Without Men* (2009), a rewriting of Shahrnush Parsiour's magic realist novel. In works like *Passage* (2001), commissioned by Philip Glass, she relies on preverbal language and deconstructs binary opposites through nonlinear and multidirectional dialectic messages. Her aim is to allow "more open interpretations" in a global context and to try to explain "how an artist who comes from and remains interested in the resources of another culture can make work that contributes to a broader culture" (Matt 2000: 19).

Also between two worlds and two languages is Mona Hatoum, a well-known London-based artist born in Lebanon to Palestinian exiles. She employs unusual combinations of techniques and media in her work, where this hybridity stands for ideological and cultural multiplicity (Minissale 2013: xxix). Hatoum reflects on home, exile, and the loss of her mother tongue in *Measures of Distance* (1988), a 15-minute single-channel video layering the visual and the aural. The viewer sees excerpts in Arabic and listens to the artist's voice reading her mother's letters[9] in an almost completely flat monotone, in English. This is the language in which she translates her excerpts that talk of fragmentation and the painful sense of not knowing where one belongs, while the spectator views Arabic handwriting as a partially alienating visual text.

Some of Hatoum's multilingual pieces remind the visitor of the simultaneous poems of the Dadaists. Like many other media artists, Hatoum's work combines linguistic multimodality and multimediality, written and oral language, different languages and translation, understood not only as a way of communicating meaning from one language to another but in a much more comprehensive way between different semiotic systems, media, and cultures. These are media artworks "that both present and transform acts of translation—as shifts and volatile movements between different languages and linguistic modalities, and between different media and cultures" (Benthien 2019: 39). Claudia Benthien (2019) offers an excellent analysis of *Measures of Distance* in different publications (regarding the role of translation in this work, see also Benthien *et al.* 2019: 202–204).[10] She concludes that in this artwork, "translation takes place aesthetically in several ways: the artist translates Arabic letters, represented visually, into spoken English communication that can be heard at the same time—a monolog superimposed onto an Arabic dialogue" (Benthien 2019: 55).

Benthien gives other examples of media artwork created with different languages and different systems of writing by Young-Hae Chang Heavy Industries and Danica Dakić. Multilingualism is in fact present in the artist collective, Young-Hae Chang Heavy Industries (YHCHI), a web-art group consisting of the Korean artist and translator Young-Hae Chang and the American poet Marc Voge. They create online art, which can be viewed at www.yhchang.com, in more than twenty languages, and juxtapose different scripts, for example Latin versus Korean[11] and different fonts with a view to highlighting the materiality and spatiality of script. Their artwork is full of references to film and literature as in *But Down the Door Again!*, *Dakota,* or *Samsung Means to Come* (1999), in English, French, and Korean. *So you made it. What do you know. Congratulations and welcome!* (2017) is an exhibition that features two floor-to-ceiling screens displaying a one-hour loop of seven videos, with one screen showing the text in English and the other in Korean, Swedish, Japanese, Arabic, Spanish, and Chinese (for an analysis of the group's use of multilingualism see Benthien 2019: 43–48).

As observed by Benthien (2019: 51–55), the work of the Bosnian-German artist, Danica Dakić, is also in this same line. *Blaues Auge* (1996) is a reflection on the isolation during the war in Yugoslavia, as told through newspaper cuttings of words and images that paradoxically did not facilitate communication. This highlights the opacity of the news provided by the media.

Autoportrait (1999) is a single-channel video production in which the figure portrayed has no eyes but two mouths, one speaking in German and the other in Bosnian. These two discourses, which are not synchronized, reproduce two fairy tales in voices from all over the world. The differences in content between the translations of the Bosnian and German versions of the oral narrations are extremely pertinent. Since the two mouths speak in different languages, they say different things.

> The two oral narrations of fairy tales differ significantly, which is apparent even if the viewer cannot speak Bosnian or German, e.g., due to the recitation of a list of different languages in the Bosnian version . . . a passage that is not found in the German tale. The artist, speaking simultaneously in two languages, demonstrates that both "mouths" have something different to say.
>
> (Benthien 2019: 55)

In *Touched* (2010), Dakić shows the connections between language and music, spectacle, and the legal system. In *Isola Bella* (2007–2008) she translates alienation and silence through masks and a character that does not speak English. These are "narrated worlds",

> independent narratives that may have been handed down in their respective cultures and linguistic communities (or written by the artist herself). This situation of 'double-voicedness' . . . in which one must listen to both tales simultaneously, becomes recognizable as a fundamental disruption, out of which only singular moments of transparency emerge.
>
> (Benthien 2019: 55)

In this context, the Turkish artist, Kutlug Ataman, is also relevant. For instance, his *Mesopotamian Dramaturgies* series. *English as a Second Language* and *The Complete Works of William Shakespeare* (2009) reflect on the problem of communication in the world. Ataman specifically focuses on the role of writing and the word when he translates Western canonical works and rewrites them in another context. His intention is not for them to be represented on stage but rather for them to be presented as pure Eastern calligraphy. His objective is to

> further question modernity as a phenomenon of failed translation in making the failure a performative creative act. Whereas the former presents Turkish youth reading out aloud the rhymes of Edward Lear, the latter is a four-and-a-half-minute projection of the handwritten transcription of all of Shakespeare's plays. While the former treats English as lingua franca of the modern . . . the latter performs an extratextual translation, or perhaps a cross-cultural transfiguration, from text to calligraphic image.
>
> (Çakırlar 2013: 704)

Cildo Meireles, a very committed Latin American artist, also deals with translation in works such as *Babel*, a huge installation composed of seven hundred radios all turned on at the same time and emitting badly tuned frequencies in different languages. As a critical metaphor of globalization, this work expresses the tension between the global and the local and confuses the viewer because of the indecipherable noises and hundreds of voices coming from the radios, with different accents and pronunciations from a multitude of cities throughout the world. The artist uses these voices to condemn the difficult coexistence of difference in the same spatial area. He emphasizes the existence of abstract borders that permits the entry of information that filters ideologies (Di Paola 2017).

These examples and many others (i.e., see Campbell and Vidal 2019) "challenge the word-based model of 'the reading'" (Apter 2007: 149). They show that translating outward is an adventure in the experience of different languages:

> What if translation is an adventure not in meaning but in readerly consciousness and the *experience* of language? What if reading is looked upon not as a process of interpreting, or extracting meaning from, text but as a process of existential/experiential self-coordination or self-orchestration? What if translation is not a test of comprehension but of the fruitfulness of our inability to comprehend? . . . experiences evaporate unless we know how to name them; language becomes the indispensable repository of our collective experience . . . Translation must be allowed to open up and develop its own multimedial discursive space. It ceases to be a discipline ('translation studies') and becomes a philosophical enquiry into its own functions and possible relationships with the translator's being-in-the-world.
>
> (Scott in Campbell and Vidal 2019: 88)

On the other hand, within the art world, many exhibitions revolve around the concept of translation.[12] In all these cases and in many more (cf., Vidal 2017), the art world shows that it understands that concepts and challenges currently engaging translation (globalization, cosmopolitanism, borders, movement, travel, identities, fragmentation, migrations, *inter alia*) are also key to contemporary artistic practice (Iannicielo 2018; Tello 2016; Rizzo 2019). This is eloquent proof of Bal's idea (2006: 29), that no concept is immovable and that concepts travel between disciplines, communities, and historical periods. It is thus already possible to speak of an epistemology of visual translation in and from the artistic and visual field (Di Paola 2018a). This is largely thanks to the development of visual studies, which, as previously discussed, has generated a context for the relationship between the arts and the shift from one language to another. Translation can thus be understood in the sense of Mieke Bal and Joanne Morra (2007) as a fundamental way of looking in the visual and cultural practices of any discipline to address concepts such as globalization, diasporas, and identities.

In fact, globalization has fully impacted the world of art (Guasch 2018; Weibel 2017; Fillitz *et al.* 2012; Elkins 2007, 2020) because artistic production today reaches Biennials and other international artistic encounters. This implies an urgent reterritorialization, decentralization, and reorientation of art, and its Eurocentric and Western assumptions. New strategies are needed to face the political and aesthetic but also the linguistic and intercultural challenges facing a now global art that necessarily has to rewrite traditional approaches to the history of art.

Accordingly, the biennials of Johannesburg and Havana, the prelude to the "biennials of the South" (e.g., those of Istanbul, Dakar, Gwangju, and others), are references "for exhibitions and biennials after the 1980s based on global exchanges and the incorporation of territories traditionally excluded from contemporary art" (Garrido 2017: 74l). However, it was the *Magiciens de la Terre* exhibition (1989) that constituted the beginning of a global vision of art that despite the controversy that it generated (Guasch 2018: 90ff), put in check "old geographical borders and reclaiming narratives of place and displacement. In other words, new cultural practices that transfigure the relationship between the global and the local and articulate the discourse of difference" (Guasch 2018: 7).[13]

Consequently, books such as *Contemporary Art and the Museum* (2007) appear to answer the new questions posed by this globalization of art in the traditional museum space. This is a way of overcoming Eurocentrism and reflecting on museums as "contested sites where the representation of a given culture becomes a political issue" (Buddensieg and Weibel 2007: 6). More recently, many publications focus on the issue of how official powers create representations of those who have no voice, especially refugees and migrants (Saloni 2011; Bal and Hernández Navarro 2011; Marciniak and Tyler 2014; Pultz Moslund *et al.* 2015; Schimanski and Wolfe 2017; Ring Petersen 2017). In contrast, others are centered on the images that have been generated of migrants (Bischoff *et al.* 2010; Papastergiadis 2012; Demos 2013; Steyn and Stamselberg 2014; Sheren 2015; Ianniciello 2018; Schramm *et al.* 2019). All these books and many others represent an important change in the vision of migrants. They raise the question of how public powers and institutions have rewritten and post-translated the migrant, and how they have generated certain images, but not others, which have given rise to concrete discourses about them.

In contrast, other scholars demonstrate that another narrative is possible. For example, Alexandra Rizzo (2019) shows the concern of the art world about migration and refugees and Bertacco and Vallorani (2021: 17, 87–110) focus on visual representations of migration as translated texts where "the gaze is also influenced by the colonial semiosis . . . More directly than words, images raise the issue of a biopolitics of language". Federica Mazzara (2019) analyzes the work of a series of artists who focus on immigration in Lampedusa: "the impact of migrants as others on the Mediterranean island of Lampedusa, paying particular attention to the strategies of representation in the public discourse" and she concludes that art can offer another look at those "on the move with their power to cross, subvert and de-legitimate borders and stereotypes" (Mazzara 2019: 2). Thus, the potential of art to resist the status quo by criticizing the culture of consensus that is generated by politics is recognized—as acknowledged by Mazzara (2019:16), "there is a need to disagree, to live in tension with one another, and art can make this tension visible".

Art addresses issues in which translation is immersed. These issues include schizophrenia between the defense of the local versus the global in the defense of indigenous[14] artistic practices. It also highlights issues of identity in the context of international flows, diasporas, and migrations, with nationalisms and ethnicity (Elkins *et al.* 2010), the deconstruction of historical discourses based on dichotomies, hierarchical organization and centers of power, to favor "transnational, pluralistic, horizontal, poly-phonic and multidimensional historical-artistic narratives" (Guasch 2016: 21). Considerably less focus is placed on the extent to which globalization affects the contemporary art market, as analyzed in the three-volume series by Hans Belting and Peter Weibel, titled *Global Art and the Museum*.

As with all products of globalization, art leaves the context for which it was created. Consequently, problems of understanding arise from questions such as "how to negotiate unequal temporalities, or how each subject is positioned within history and its past" (Guasch 2016: 20). The geography of art changed after the end of the cold war. New York, London, Paris, and Berlin gave way to the emergence of new non-European spaces that high-light the global turn of contemporary art after colonization, the migration of artistic contexts, the end of the traditional canon, and the emergence of new representation strategies. And all this needs to be translated.

In this regard, it is worth noting the exhibition held at the German museum ZKM Center for Art and Media in Karlsruhe in 2011 titled *The Global Contemporary: Art Worlds After 1989* (which resulted in the publication, *The Global Contemporary and the Rise of New Art Worlds*). Also relevant is *Lost in Translation: New Biographies of Artists* because it incorporates works that address the issue of cultural translation. The exhibition focuses on the geo-political transformations of globalization and their influence on the art world, on the conditions of its production, its dissemination, and the working methods of artists, as well as the production and reception of their work. Art is today an "art of transnational transitionality" (Smith 2013: 189). As pointed out by Peter Weibel, it is an exhibition that, in contrast to the traditional dichotomous idea of inclusion/exclusion, which gives rise to the well-known clash of civilizations (Huntington 1996) and the concept of confluence (Trojanow and Hoskoté 2007), rewrites and translates. The contemporary world is today part of a global rewriting program:

we are experiencing an epoch of rewriting programs: rewriting art history, rewriting political and economic history on a global scale.

Translations and transfers from one culture to another, in a multilateral and multipolar world, no longer create the hegemony of an international art, but the reevaluation of the local and the regional. We are witnessing the reentry of forgotten and unforeseen parts of geography and history, we experience how historic concepts and events are reenacted. Contemporary art and the contemporary world are part of a global rewriting program. We observe how Indian art rewrites European art and how European art rewrites Indian art, how European art rewrites Asian art and how Asian art rewrites North American art. We are witnessing a new cartography of art in the making.

(Weibel 2017: 20)

Art shows how global culture and economic transformations rewrite the historical, ethnic, and cultural metamorphoses that are taking place. From our perspective, what Weibel calls the new cartographies of art are post-translations of the technologies, economies, policies, cultures, and artistic forms of the global and cosmopolitan era, thanks to which "the confluences and influences of cultures are articulated" (*ibid.*). For Weibel, art is that magnifying glass that allows us to look at these global rewriting processes, given that art is a reflection of society, and life in society is a constant rewriting:

The idea of rewriting is based on the assumption that every system consists of a finite number of elements and of a limited number of rules as to how these elements are connected and can be sequenced. These rules are called rewriting rules. In language, they constitute a grammar. In society, they can be called codes of behaviour, or marriage laws, or traffic laws, or rules for cooking. If we consider society as a system, then it is possible to apply the idea of rewriting programs to it. It is also the case that rewritings can take place in society. What has been happening in nature for millions of years is a constant process of rewriting. . . . So what we have been calling integration, assimilation, inclusion, and exclusion are, from this perspective, merely processes of rewriting.

(Weibel 2017: 12)

Consequently, this transnational art in constant transition and movement requires linguistic and intercultural translation and mediation. This is clear in exhibitions such as the one curated by Yu Yeon Kim, titled *Translated Acts: Performance and Body Art from East Asia. 1990–2001*, whose catalogue also highlights the urgency of translating two aspects: "the articulation of cultural identity, historical legacy, and inner expression into performance— and the second the extension of the body and performative action into other mediums, such as photography, video and digital or networked space" (Kim 2001: 13). Also relevant is the work of the Croatian artist Mladen Stilinovic titled *An artist who cannot speak English is not an artist* (1994), which is a critique of the imperialism of English on the Internet and in a world that is only apparently global.

Theorization on this issue began more than a decade ago in the pioneering publication *Journal of Visual Culture*, with Mieke Bal's (2003) controversial article, "Visual Essentialism and the Object of Visual Culture". Still another example is the 2007 monograph titled *Acts of Translation* with contributions from translation scholars such as Emily Apter and Lawrence Venuti along with others from the world of art. The editors, Mieke Bal and Joanne Morra, understand translation as an indispensable concept that should be present in any debate on contemporary visual and cultural practices:

> Today translation is gaining ground as a crucial trope, idea, concept, metaphor and mode of interpretation within discussions of international visual and cultural practices. Art historians, cultural and literary critics, philosophers and psychoanalysts are turning to modern and contemporary theories of translation in order to consider visual, historical, social and subjective transformations.
>
> (Bal and Morra 2007: 5)

And this is so because the most recent translation theories understand this activity as a way of looking at the globalized world, as a way of being and feeling, and as a way of incorporating issues of gender, race, borders, marginalities, and all those concepts that need to be considered for an ethical reflection on the complexity of today's societies:

> Benefiting from and paralleling these contributions are the recent engagements with translation within art history, visual culture studies, film, media and cultural studies. For instance, translation is deployed as a way of interrogating and understanding the epistemological, ontological and philosophical possibilities provoked by a work of art (Bal 2002; Morra 2000; Shapiro 1997; Steyn 1996). It is integral to recent discussions on diaspora, exile and the construction of the other within analyses of modern and contemporary visual culture practices (Bhabha 1997; Maharaj and Papastergiadis 1999; Naficy 2001). Translation provides a discursive context for discussions about globalization, and the necessity and impossibility of intercultural and international dialogue.
>
> (Bal and Morra 2007: 6)

At that time, concepts such as translating outward or post-translation had not yet emerged. However, the definition of translation proposed by the editors is similar since they describe it as mobile, fluid, unlimited, interdisciplinary, and open:

> We are using the term "intermedial translation" to mean, quite simply, translating across media. To "translate across" is to work within discourses and practices of intertextuality, intersemiotics and interdisciplinarity, which can lead to movements across genres, media, bodies of knowledge and subjects. More figuratively, translating across is concerned with the marginal, the gaps, fissures and contradictions of working in the interstices between these various boundaries. As will become clear, these issues are intimately concerned with matters of intercultural translation, and require us to think and work across nations, ethnicities, subjectivities, histories, politics and ethics.
>
> (Bal and Morra 2007: 7)

Translating outward means translating from hospitality but not from "hostipitality", because *hostis* and *hospes* are two concepts that are easily confused when we impose our view of the world on the other (Derrida 1997/2000, 2000). When we do not let him/her look. A good example of this situation is the video of Mieke Bal and Shahram Entekhabi titled *Lost in Space* (2005), which is about Daryush, an Iranian, and his difficulties with English. He misses speaking his own language because he fails to identify with the new language as well as with the values of the society to which he has immigrated.

The outward translator is aware of the need to act on the basis of new models and methodologies to face the asymmetries between strong and weak languages, new hybrid mestizo identities and the political and ethical issues thus generated. All of this obliges us to consider new questions before starting to translate. These questions include whether it is really plausible to say today that languages are pure, not to mention how we should translate a text constructed with images, colors, sounds, noises, bodies.

Notes

1. Wassili Kandinski, one of the greatest exponents of abstraction, also mixes different languages in his art. He elaborates "a grammar of abstract visual language" capable of constructing narratives and talks about the "writing" of the pictorial text in books such as *Concerning the Spiritual in Art* (1911) and *Point and Line to Plane* (1926). In the latter he does so by using the word "translation" as a necessary process between different fields.
2. A considerable number of books and articles have been published on *conceptual art*, a widely debated term. In this regard, Alberro and Stimson (2000) provide

key documents and statements by artists and critics. Nonetheless, contemporary art has been using words for decades and many artists anticipated a way of representing reality and a way of translating outward as moving through different disciplines. For instance, John Baldessari's text-paintings and photographs (Diack 2020) create artwork with texts, thus ironically defining painting with a text. In *What Is Painting* (1968), he states that "art is a creation for the eye and can only be hinted at with words". He uses many media, including photography, video, paintings, books, film, and drawings, but is fascinated by visual and written language. He explores the connections between word and image in his video performances, *I am Making Art* (1971) ("reminiscent of Dadaist 'movement poems'", Benthien *et al.* 2019: 53) or *Xylophone* (1972), as well as the ambiguous relationship between textual and visual components in another of his text-paintings, *Tips for Artists Who Want to Sell* (1966–1968). There are also interactions between image and text in his series *Wrong* (1966–1968), *Goya Series* (i.e., *Not so that you could tell it* or *And,* 1997) and *Prima Facie* (2005). Many conceptual artists insist on their political position. These artists include Michael Baldwin, Terry Atkinson, or Ian Burn, members of *Art & Language*. With its complement in the *Art & Language* group (Bailey 2016), conceptual art places itself outside the aesthetic and favors idea and concept (Combalía 2005). Starting from Duchamp and keeping in mind the diversity of artistic objects covered by the adjective "conceptual", one immediately thinks of artists such as Carl André, Marcel Broodthaers, George Brecht, On Kawara, Barbara Kruger, Jenny Holzer, and others already mentioned. Also relevant are works such as *Red Square, White Letters* (1963) by Sol Lewitt, Hans Haacke's surveys, Mary Kelly's *Post-Partum Document*, gestures (which review Klein's monochromes or Pollock's actions from a feminist perspective) in the Perpetual Fluxus Festival of 1965 of Shigeko Kubota and her "vagina paintings", the actions within Walter de Maria's Land Art or Robert Smithson, the exhibition organized by Douglas Crimp in 1977 for the New York Artists Space titled *Pictures*, *Arte Povera* or the collaborations between Sherrie Levine and Louise Lawler in the project *A Picture is No Substitute for Anything*. There is also *a: a novel*, by Andy Warhol, based on the idea of non-creativity and non-originality so characteristic of all his works. All of them and many more translate the world through images and words, travelling between disciplines. They all share a critical approach to the referential value of representation.

3. Although language is part of conceptual art, very few publications approach the role of the artist as translator. Terry Smith, a conceptual artist himself, deals with the role of translation, from a Benjaminian and Derridean perspective, in several Art & Language exhibitions in an article (Smith 1990) and most recently in a book (Smith 2017). Before Smith, and suspicious of his claims on translation and his ideas on Art & Language, Ian Burn, also involved with Art & Language, was interested in translation: "his own work on translation . . . drew on 'a wide range of sources, from John Cage and Jasper Johns to Wittgenstein, Barthes and further.' Burn is correct that the work *Soft-Tape*, which he developed together with Mel Ramsden in 1966, predates Smith's exhibitions by roughly a decade, and he is also correct that many of the ideas about translation advanced in it provide highly germane background to the Art & Language work that Smith did in Australia and New Zealand" (Bailey in Smith 2017: 13). Another interesting book "on the material qualities, technologies, and affiliations of writing identified variously as literature and as art" is Andersson's (2018: 4), who for example

addresses Broodthaers' art as a body of work comprised of language, generated through practices of appropriation, transcription, translation, redaction, and repetition". The volume also deals with translation in many other chapters.

4. For a discussion of the abstract use of the body as a new visual language in her *Sex Pictures* from Kristeva's notion of "ejection" see Colby 2012.

5. Campbell and Vidal lead an interesting research project with other translators and artists: AIIRC Experiential Translation Network https://experientialtranslation.net/2021/07/09/etn-holds-its-first-symposium/. SIG Leader Intersemiotic Translation and Cultural Literacy: Cultural Literacy in Europe: http://cleurope.eu/activities/sigs/. See also Campbell and González 2018.

6. The volume includes texts on the role of translation in hybrid contexts, displacement and diaspora, globalization, and so on. Also, chapters on how translation is often constructed through the senses, as in the case of the deaf and blind human rights activist, Helen Keller, who argues that language "manifests across the whole spectrum of the senses" (Williamson 2019: 15). Or Amanda Baggs, a non-verbal autistic blogger who "in her video *In My Language* portrays a world of deep sensory non-linguistic dialogue with everything surrounding her, a language that would be unfathomable to most of us reading this book" (*ibid.*, p. 14).

7. This performance was given in the Guggenheim Museum in Bilbao (it was first shown in the Guggenheim in New York) as part of the exhibition *Arte y China después de 1989: el teatro del mundo* (2018), causing huge controversy on the part of animal activists because it reached the limits of what the West accepts as animal maltreatment: two pigs with Western and Chinese characters stamped all over their skin are seen copulating on a floor covered in loose pages from works of Chinese and Western literature.

8. https://noma.org/qa-shirin-neshat-portrays-iranian-culture-and-personal-memory-in-photography-and-film/

9. The epistolary novel subgenre is used by other media artists such as the Indian Zarina Hashmi, who also explores the written word, for instance, in *Letters from Home* (2004), eight monochromatic woodblock and metal-cut prints, produced with original letters written in Urdu.

10. Other excellent examples of multilingual media artists who use language as a material in itself, mix different media and voices, and experiment with translations can be found in Benthien *et al.* 2019. This book is an excellent contribution to interart studies (Fischer-Lichte 2016), a field that blurs the boundaries between different art disciplines such as dance, film, music, visual arts, and so on.

11. Some media artists simultaneously use different language systems such as Shelly Silver in her digital film *5 lessons and 9 questions about Chinatown* (2009), a work that "combines spoken and written Mandarine, Cantonese and English" with photographs, maps and cartoons (Benthien *et al.* 2019: 75). For an analysis of the influence of literary genres and of literary works on many media artists see Benthien *et al.* 2019: 111–271.

12. Examples include the following: *Translaziuns Paradoxien Malenclegïentschas* in Zürich (2008); *Bad Translation* at the Crate Space in Margate (2009); *Tarjama/Translation*, (2009) at the Queens Museum of Art in New York; the *A Collector's Album of Traders, Traitors, Translators, and Experientialists* project of Cabinet Magazine in the Sharjah Biennial (2010); *Translating as a Structuring Principle*, at the Gentili Apri in Berlin (2010); *Translation is a Mode*, at the Kunstraum Niederiesterreich in Vienna (2010); *Found in Translation*, organized

by the Guggenheim of New York (2011); *Found in Translation, Chapter L* at the Luxembourg Casino in Luxembourg (2011–2012); *The Spiral and the Square: Exercises on Translatability*, at the Bonniers Konsthall in Stockholm (2011) with the theme, Haroldo de Campos's idea of translation and "transcreation"; and the novel *Avalovara* (1973), by the also Brazilian Osman Lins. Other important events include the second Tehran Curatorial Symposium, titled "The Curator as Translator" (Tehran, January 5–7, 2019); the conference, "Babel Global: los vértigos del infinito" (Universitat de Barcelona, October 25–26, 2018); and "Après Babel, traduire" (2016), at the MUCEUM in Marseille, (see Dot 2019: 12–13).

13. The importance of this exhibition was seen 25 years later with the remake of *Magiciens de la terre* held at the Centre Georges Pompidou in July 2014, where it was made clear, through collections of letters, publications, photographs, and debates that the Eurocentric Western look was no longer dominant.
14. In this regard, see for instance the analysis made in a book like *Global Studies* of artistic manifestations in Zimbabwe, Indonesia, China, or Afghanistan, among others (cf., Fillitz *et al.* 2012).

4 Concluding Remarks

The end of the twentieth century witnessed various redefinitions of translation, most of which were culturally determined and power-related. Translation was sorely in need of innovative approaches and new interpretations because of the widespread dissatisfaction with traditional views that conceived translation work as an objective and empirical enterprise. Within this perspective, translators were supposed to be impartial and invisible even though this was evidently not true.

Thanks to the incorporation of concepts such as manipulation, ideology, power, and asymmetry, Translation Studies has managed to considerably broaden its horizons, and is now actively engaged with our globalized world. New descriptions of translation argue that "since there can be no definitive reading there can obviously be no definitive translation . . . [we] conceive translation as interpretation and hence as rewriting *and* creation of a new 'original'" (Bassnett 2014b: 152, 153).

In the twenty-first century, translation has become an important venue for raising questions pertaining to representation as well as to the linguistic construction of reality. Today, "translation seems to be everywhere. . . . This idea of translation as an essential factor in contemporary communication repositions translation and moves it from a marginal activity to one that occupies center stage" (Bassnett 2014c: 55). Translation is no longer understood as the mere representation of an original. It is now regarded as a Deleuzian map, as the production of heteroglossic texts in which the translator's voice must also be heard. The translator "must always employ more than just the visual sense: a poem can be read, spoken, heard, performed as well as acted out, smelled (by association) or felt. And, of course, the same goes for a painting, a film or dance, etc." (Campbell and Vidal 2019: 3).

Translation has now begun to look beyond the linguistic and the literary to better understand "this new intercultural and intersemiotic age of translation" (Gentzler 2017: 217). Decades ago, Lawrence Weiner suggested that everyone should "learn to read [not see] Art" (in Welish 1996: 11). And in her keynote delivered at Dartington College of Arts in 1996, Caroline Bergvall (Bergvall 1996 in Andersson 2018: 89, 91, 92), on Performance Writing, refers to Marcel Broodthaers as an artist who chose to locate

> a writerly activity not primarily on the page but in objects and spatial constructs . . . it is a shift in attitude with regards to what defines the writerly. . . . So where does the text start or end? . . . Where does a text start? Where does it not end?

Given the transversality of disciplines, the artistranslator should be able to answer these questions by shifting between different semiotic spaces of art and translation. S/he must be passionately concerned with the different ways of representing and being represented.

Translators are obviously interested in language. This statement is so self-evident that it is almost a *boutade*. However, we currently inhabit a hybrid, multimodal, multicultural, cosmopolitan, and global world, which, above all, is asymmetrical. It is not sufficient for translators to merely be interested in language. It is just as important (if not more so) for them to be interested in *languages*, languages that include looks, sounds, colors, and sensations. In short, they must be utterly fascinated by all the representations of the world created in *any* semiotic system, because today "all media deploy more than one modality" (Bal in Elleström 2021: v).

New ideas on translation are now closer to those of well-known artists who over the years have been rewriting with images, colors, bodies, forms, and sounds. For instance, in the early 1950s, the neo-Dadaist artist, Robert Rauschenberg, created a series of white paintings whose image was the spectator's shadow. These white paintings were followed by a series of totally black paintings. However, the originals for both series were the entirely white paintings by Lucio Fontana in 1946 and the first monochromes painted by Yves Klein in 1950.

Like John Cage, Rauschenberg worked for Merce Cunningham's ballet company (as a performer and stage designer). His aesthetic philosophy was also based on that of Cage, whom he had met in North Carolina. Cage's idea was to shift the spectators' focus so that they would open up to their surroundings and gain more self-awareness. In *Silence*, for example, he claims that music is not an attempt to understand something that is said because if it were said, the sound would transmit the form of the words (Cage 1961: 10). Music is simply attention to the activity of sounds. Rauschenberg *translated* Cage when he painted his huge *Barge* in 1962, a kind of dream in which the viewer is invited to participate. The picture is "a flux of images which are not necessarily fixed and immutable. Cage remarks on the 'quality of the encounter' between Rauschenberg and the materials he uses" (Lucie-Smith 1984: 124).

Cage's practice has been analyzed in light of Walter Benjamin's notion of translation—and Cage himself can be regarded as a kind of translator (Saletnik 2012). Saletnik sees Cage's work in sound, text, and image as "modalities of expression". He elaborates upon Benjamin's view of translation as demonstrating "the kinship of languages". According to Saletnik, Cage's work exemplifies "how translation as a posture of inquiry may aid us in moving toward interdisciplinary understanding in the humanities" (Saletnik 2012: 76):

> Like a translation and its original, we can understand Cage's individual works more fully when approaching them pluralistically, enacting a relational—even analytical—dynamic akin to the way Benjamin and others might encourage us to consider the act of translating. In this regard, we can posit Cage's music, writing, and visual art as reflecting upon one another—even as enriching one another.
>
> (Saletnik 2012: 76)

As explained in more detail elsewhere (Vidal 2017), both the white pictures and *4'3"* can be understood as translations because they are texts that rewrite the real and reveal the different ways of looking at those who observe them and/or listen to them. The centrality of language in all these works is a symptom of a transition from the sign as a representation of the world to an image of the world as a textual sign. This is what Bassnett and Johnston's "outward turn", Gentzler's "post-translation", and Campbell and Vidal's "experiential translation" propose. Iain Chambers (2017: 56) states:

> Thinking with music and the visual arts is not simply to seek an alternative catalogue of subaltern and subversive replies to Western hegemony. It is also to consider instances of art working the elaboration of counter-intuitive critical spaces. Seeing and sounding modernity in a different key is to cut up and disperse a unilateral framing of the world.

Curators have recently begun to show interest in the conjunction between art and translators. For example, Emily Butler is now focusing on artists as mis-translators and on how the curator can avoid being a secondary translator. It is thus no surprise that she writes about Nalini Malani, referring to her as a translator. Malani rewrites conflict from a feminist perspective using images and recontextualizing the quotes of different writers. Not surprisingly, one of her exhibitions is called *Twice Upon a Time* (2014). Malini's art "is never monocultural" (Bal 2015: 55) since she rewrites myths and post-translates narratives:

> —*twice* upon a time. The title denotes an aesthetic of the fairy tale, that quintessential narrative genre, but the distortion ("twice") refers to the incorrigible pressure of ideology that narratives tend to convey. This fairy tale has neither a happy ending nor an indeterminate future (happily ever after). It remains in the middle of times as well as cultures: age-old, never gone away. Hence the need to embed these stories into an archive from which we, as viewers, must select and re-compose our own narratives.
>
> (Bal 2015: 55)

In *Can you Hear Me?* Butler argues that Nalini Malani explores the possibilities of language from a translator's perspective. She rewrites artworks from the past and post-translates them. Thus, her pieces "shatter the belief of a continuous or a single version of history by offering an incessant and fragmented stream of voices, ideas and images, building a picture of a shared and layered writing of it" (Butler 2020: 63). Her post-translations re-tell images (Bal 2016: 49, 2018: 66ff) and highlight overlooked stories, such as those of Medea or Cassandra:

> In the manner of a translator, Malani uses different modes of expression—written, drawn, spoken, to transmit knowledge in another form. . . . She asks us to consider alternative methods of communication, urging us to pause, watch, listen and think. Who is speaking? What is being said? What can we hear? What can we learn from this? How can we listen better?
>
> (Butler 2020: 68)

Borges was probably never more accurate than when he stated that translation completes the original, broadens its meanings, opens up new interpretations, and asks questions that generate other questions. Translation also reads the original text and is a journey to a rugged landscape with misty views, which is, however, worth exploring. Not a trip free of obstacles, it traverses a difficult though rewarding cartography that replaces strengths with thresholds in which to translate. Translation is a third space, a vernacular cosmopolitanism (Bhabha 1994) that gives rise to insinuations, promiscuous itineraries, without limits or borders, capable of looking to explore rather than to exploit the other (Bielsa 2016a, 2016b). This is translating without dominating, translation that admits distance, outside oneself, within each other, and in both places at the same time. It means looking at other geographies that enrich us by rejecting that false legitimacy manifest in grammar, limited to the impregnability of the safe one-way direction. Translation thus becomes an intersemiotic encounter that "can serve as an awareness-raising tool to promote empathy and cultural literacy by going beyond verbal expressions of difference through embodied experience" (Campbell and Vidal 2019: 31).

In today's world, translating bears little or no resemblance to walking over a sturdy well-designed overpass to safely reach the other side. Translating is more like crossing a gorge on a flimsy suspension bridge made of fraying rope that perilously sways in the wind with the translator's every step. Translating is a continuous source of questionable and revisable realities, and precisely for this reason, it is so exciting.

This is a far cry from the notion of similarity and from the Platonic cave where the universal fixed Idea reigns supreme. It is more in line with the Rortian linguistic turn, which replaced the Kantian transcendental subject with the system based on the Humboldtian conception of language, where meaning has preeminence over reference. Similarly, these new views on translation do not foreground the object, but rather its systems of representation with all of their conventions and biases. Consequently, they highlight the conditions, archeology, and genealogy of language. Even more important, they prioritize the languages that contemplate the past, present, and future of these diverse semiotic systems now used to transmit texts in our culture. Every translation is thus a rereading, a rewriting and "an interpretation":

> Translation, in other words, is never reducible to its common definition, "putting a work into another language"; after the cultural turn in translation studies in the 1990s and the current "textual turn," nearly all translation scholarship now acknowledges the many complications that proliferate around an act of translation. But the one consistently accessible site of transformative agency—what we can always hear working through these compounded complexities—is the translator's voice.
>
> (Coldiron 2016: 311)

In her introduction to a volume of the *Philological Quarterly*, Coldiron never writes "translations and originals" but "translations and their prior texts" (*ibid.:* 315). This could also be applied to Cindy Sherman's translations and to many of the preceding examples since "translations are always more than simple linguistic transfers, reflecting both particular interventions and broad trends" (*ibid.*: 322).

This new approach to translation means that reaching outward to other disciplines, such as contemporary art, is an extremely exciting and enriching endeavor. An outward turn in Translation Studies clearly reveals the advantages of an image-to-word translation in which it is possible to move across genres, media, and bodies of knowledge. This approach facilitates a concern with the marginal and makes it possible to take into account the gaps, fissures, and contradictions of working in the interstices between the various boundaries.

This ultimately obliges us to go "beyond a basic understanding of translation as a word-to-word process, and consider it a poetic, political and experiential mode" (Bal and Morra 2007: 7; also, Campbell and Vidal 2019). To paraphrase Benjamin, translation is "a mode of writing that works against codification, imitation, derivation, and stasis" and instead "proposes a philosophy of language in which translation does not serve the original but liberates and releases its potential" (Bal and Morra 2007: 5). The translator's gaze is translated into an "intense looking . . . which includes the full immersion of the translator in the text, with eyes, ears, skin, nose, limbs and heart" (Campbell and Vidal 2019: 3). Translation thus becomes a way of questioning the dominant paradigm of reading in favor of the analysis of the visual and non-verbal gaps between words, to translate "the reading" into "the looking" (Apter 2007; Clarke 2007).

In the end, translation is simply a way to allow the other to look. It is a way to ask, "Who are we? Who have we been while we have been looking?"

References

Adami, Elisabetta. 2016. "Multimodality", in Ofelia García *et al.*, eds. *The Oxford Handbook of Language and Society*. Oxford: Oxford University Press, 451–472.

Adorno, Theodor. 1970/2002. *Aesthetic Theory*. London: Continuum. Trans. Robert Hullot-Kentor.

Aguiar, Daniella, and João Queiroz. 2015. "From Gertrude Stein to Dance. Repetition and Time in Intersemiotic Translation", *Dance Chronicle* 38: 1–29.

Ahrens, Barbara *et al.*, eds. 2021. *Translation—Kunstkommunikation—Museum. Translation—Art Communication—Museum*. Berlin: Frank & Timme.

Akcan, Esra. 2018. "Writing a Global History through Translation: An Afterword on Pedagogical Perspectives", *Art in Translation* 10, 1: 136–142.

Akcan, Esra. 2012. *Architecture in Translation: Germany, Turkey and the Modern House*. Durham and London: Duke University Press.

Alberro, Alexander, and Patricia Norvell, eds. 2001. *Recording Conceptual Art*. Berkeley: University of California Press.

Alberro, Alexander, and Blake Stimson. 2000. *Conceptual Art: A Critical Anthology*. Cambridge, MA: The MIT Press.

Alfer, Alexa. 2017. "Entering the Translab: Translation as Collaboration, Collaboration as Translation, and the Third Space of 'Translaboration'", *Translation and Translanguaging in Multicultural Contexts* 3, 3.

Alfer, Alexa. 2015. "Transcending Boundaries", *The Linguist* 54, 5: 26–27.

Andersson, Andrea, ed. 2018. *Postscript. Writing After Conceptual Art*. Toronto, Buffalo and London: University of Toronto Press.

Andrews, Richard. 2018. *Multimodality, Poetry and Poetics*. New York and London: Routledge.

Appadurai, Arjun, ed. 1988. *The Social Life of Things: Commodities in Cultural Perspective*. Cambridge: Cambridge University Press.

Apter, Emily. 2014. "Translation at the Checkpoint", *Journal of Postcolonial Writing* 50, 1: 56–74.

Apter, Emily. 2013. *Against World Literature: On the Politics of Untranslatability*. London: Verso.

Apter, Emily. 2007. "Untranslatable? The 'Reading' Versus the 'Looking'", *Journal of Visual Culture* 6, 1: 149–156.

Apter, Emily. 2006. *The Translation Zone: A New Comparative Literature*. Princeton: Princeton University Press.

Arduini, Stefano, and Siri Nergaard. 2011. "Translation: A New Paradigm" (2011), *Translation. A Transdisciplinary Journal*. Inaugural Issue: 8–17.

Attali, Jacques. 1985/2011. *Noise. The Political Economy of Music*. Minneapolis and London: University of Minnesota Press. Trans. Brian Massumi.

Auricchio, Laura. 2001. "Works in Translation. Ghada Amer's Hybrid Pleasures", *Art Journal* 60, 4: 26–37.

Bachmann-Medick, Doris. 2016a. *The Trans/National Study of Culture: A Translational Perspective*. Berlin and Boston: De Gruyter.

Bachmann-Medick, Doris. 2016b. *Cultural Turns. New Orientations in the Study of Culture*. Berlin and Boston: De Gruyter.

Bachmann-Medick, Doris. 2012. "Translation -A Concept and Model for the Study of Culture", in Birgit Neumann and Ansgar Nünning, eds. *Travelling Concepts for the Study of Culture*. Berlin: De Gruyter, 23–44.

Bachmann-Medick, Doris. 2009. "Introduction: The Translational Turn", *Translation Studies* 2, 1: 2–16.

Bailey, Robert. 2016. *Art & Language International. Conceptual Art Between Art Worlds*. Durham and London: Duke University Press.

Baker, Mona. 2014. "The Changing Landscape of Translation and Interpreting Studies", en Sandra Bermann and Catherine Potter, eds. *A Companion to Translation Studies*. Hoboken New Jersey: Wiley Blackwell, 15–27.

Baker, Mona. 2006. *Translation and Conflict*. New York and London: Routledge.

Bal, Mieke. 2018. "Linea Recta, Linea Perplexa: Moving through Entangled Time with Nalini Malani", in *Nalini Malani*. Rivoli-Torino: Museo D'Arte Contemporanea.

Bal, Mieke. 2016. *In Media Res. Inside Nalini Malani's Shadow Plays*. Ostfildern: Hatje Cantz.

Bal, Mieke. 2015. "Visiting Nalini Malani's Retrospective Exhibition, New Delhi, 2014", *Qui Parle* 24, 1, Fall/Winter, 31–62.

Bal, Mieke. 2006. "Conceptos viajeros en las humanidades", *Estudios Visuales* 3, enero.

Bal, Mieke. 2005. "The Commitment to Look", *Journal of Visual Culture* 2: 5–32.

Bal, Mieke. 2003. "Visual Essentialism and the Object of Visual Culture", *Journal of Visual Culture* 2, 1: 5–32.

Bal, Mieke. 2002. *Travelling Concepts in the Humanities*. Toronto: University of Toronto Press.

Bal, Mieke. 1996. *Double Exposures. The Subject of Cultural Analysis*. New York: Routledge.

Bal, Mieke. 1991. *Reading Rembrandt. Beyond the Word-Image Opposition*. Cambridge: Cambridge University Press.

Bal, Mieke. 1985/2009. *Narratology. Introduction to the Theory of Narrative*. Toronto: University of Toronto Press.

Bal, Mieke, and Miguel Ángel Hernández Navarro, eds. 2011. *Art and Visibility in Migratory Culture. Conflict, Resistance and Agency*. Amsterdam and New York: Rodopi.

Bal, Mieke, and Joanne Morra. 2007. "Acts of Translation", *Journal of Visual Culture* 6, 1: 5–11.

Barenboim, Daniel. 2008. *Everything is Connected: The Power of Music*. London: Weidenfeld and Nicholson.

Barenboim, Daniel, and Edward Said. 2003. *Parallels and Paradoxes. Explorations in Music and Society*. London: Bloomsbury.

Barnard, Malcolm. 2001. *Approaches to Understanding Visual Culture*. New York: Palgrave Macmillan.

Barthes, Roland. 1968. "L'effet de réel", *Communications* 11: 84–89.

Barthes, Roland. 1977. "The Grain of Voice", in S. Heat, ed. *Image Music Text*. London: Fontana Press. Trans. Stephen Heath.

Barthes, Roland. 1980/1992. *La cámara lúcida. Nota sobre la fotografía*. Barcelona: Paidós. Trans. Joaquim Sala-Sanahuja.

Barthes, Roland. 1982/1986. "Listening", in Richard Howard, trans. *The Responsibility of Forms: Critical Essays on Music, Art, and Representation*. Oxford: Blackwell, 245–260.

Barthes, Roland. 1986. *The Rustle of Language*. Oxford: Blackwell. Trans. Richard Howard.

Bassnett, Susan. 2017a. "Foreword", in Edwin Gentzler, ed. *Translation and Re-Writing in the Age of Post-Translation Studies*. New York and London: Routledge.

Bassnett, Susan. 2017b. "On the Direction of Translation Studies. Susan Bassnett and Anthony Pym in Dialogue", *Cultus. The Journal of Intercultural Mediation and Communication. Multilingualism, Lingua Franca or What?* 10: 145–152.

Bassnett, Susan. 2016. "The Figure of the Translator", *Journal of World Literature* 1: 299–315.

Bassnett, Susan. 2014a. "Translation Studies at a Cross-Roads", in Elke Brems, Reine Meylaerts, and Luc van Doorslaer, eds. *The Known Unknowns of Translation Studies*. Amsterdam and Philadelphia: John Benjamins, 17–28.

Bassnett, Susan. 2014b. *Translation*. London and New York: Routledge.

Bassnett, Susan. 2014c. "Variations on Translation", in Sandra Bermann and Catherine Porter, eds. *A Companion to Translation Studies*. Chichester: Wiley-Blackwell, 54–66.

Bassnett, Susan. 2011. "From Cultural Turn to Transnational Turn: A Transnational Journey", in Cecilia Alvstad, Stefan Helgesson, and David Watson, eds. *Literature, Geography, Translation. Studies in World Writing*. Cambridge: Cambridge Scholars Publishing, 67–80.

Bassnett, Susan. 2004. "Travelling and Translating", *World Literature Written in English* 40, 2: 66–76.

Bassnett, Susan, and David Johnston, eds. 2019. "The Outward Turn in Translation Studies", *The Translator. The "Outward Turn"* 25, 3: 181–188.

Bauman, Zygmunt. 2016. *Strangers at our Door*. Cambridge: Polity Press.

Bauman, Zygmunt. 2007. *Liquid Times. Living in an Age of Uncertainty*. Cambridge: Polity Press.

Bauman, Zygmunt. 2006. *Liquid Fear*. Cambridge: Polity Press.

Bauman, Zygmunt. 2000. *Liquid Modernity*. Cambridge: Polity Press.

Baynham, Mike, and Tong King Lee. 2019a. *Translation and Translanguaging*. London and New York: Routledge.

Baynham, Mike, and Tong King Lee. 2019b. "Translanguaging: A Maximalist Perspective". www.latl.leeds.ac.uk/events/translanguaging-a-maximalist-perspective/.

Benjamin, Walter. 1968. "The Task of the Translator" [first printed as introduction to a Baudelaire translation, 1923], in *Illuminations*, trans. Harry Zohn; ed. & intro. Hannah Arendt. New York: Harcourt Brace Jovanovich, 69–82.

Bennett, Karen. 2019. "Editor's Introduction", *Translation Matters* 1, 2: 1–8.

Bennett, Karen. 2007. "Words into Movement: The Ballet as Intersemiotic Translation", in Maria João Brilhante and Manuela Carvalho, eds. *Teatro e Tradução: Palcos de Encontro*. Lisbon: Colibri, 125–138.

Benthien, Claudia. 2019. "Fragile Translations. Languages of/in media Art", in Michaela Ott and Thomas Weber, eds. *Situated in Translations: Cultural Communities and Media Practices*. Transcript Verlag, 39–59.

Benthien, Claudia, Jordis Lau, and Maraike M. Marxsen. 2019. *The Literariness of Media Art*. New York and London: Routledge.

Berger, John. 1972. *Ways of Seeing*. London: Penguin.

Bergvall, Caroline. 2019. *Alisoun Sings*. New York: Nightboat Books.

Bergvall, Caroline. 2005. *Fig*. London: Salt Books.

Bergvall, Caroline. 2000. *Processing Writing: From Text to Textual Interventions*. Research Thesis. University of Plymouth.

Bergvall, Caroline. 1996. "What Do We Mean by Performance Writing?" in Andrea Andersson, ed. 2018. *Postscript. Writing After Conceptual Art*. Toronto, Buffalo and London: University of Toronto Press, 86–92.

Bermann, Sandra. 2014. "Performing Translation", in Sandra Bermann and Catherine Porter, eds. *A Companion to Translation Studies*. Chichester: Wiley-Blackwell, 285–297.

Bertacco, Simona, and Nicoletta Vallorani. 2021. *The Relocation of Culture. Translations, Migrations, Borders*. New York: Bloomsbury.

Bezemer, Jeff, and Gunther Kress. 2016. *Multimodality, Learning and Communication: A Social Semiotic Frame*. London and New York: Routledge.

Bhabha, Homi. 1994. *The Location of Culture*. London and New York: Routledge.

Bielsa, Esperança. 2016a. *Cosmopolitanism and Translation. Investigations into the Experience of the Foreign*. London and New York: Routledge.

Bielsa, Esperança. 2016b. "New Translation: Global or Cosmopolitan Connections?" *Media, Culture and Society* 38, 2: 196–211.

Bielsa, Esperança. and Dionysios Kapsaskis, eds. 2021. *The Routledge Handbook of Translation and Globalization*. London and New York: Routledge.

Bischoff, Christine *et al.* 2010. *Images of Illegalized Immigration. Towards a Critical Iconology of Politics*. Bielefeld: Verlag.

Blanchot, Maurice. 1965/1997. "The Laughter of the Gods", in *Friendship*. Stanford: Stanford University Press. 169–182. Trans. Elizabeth Rottenberg.

Blesser, Barry, and Linda-Ruth Salter. 2009. *Spaces Speak. Are You Listening?* Cambridge, MA and London: The MIT Press.

Blumczynski, Piotr. 2016. *Ubiquitous Translation.* New York: Routledge.

Boehm, Gottfried. 2011. "El giro icónico. Una carta. Correspondencia entre Gottfried Boehm and W. J. Thomas Mitchell", in Ana García Varas, ed. *Filosofía de la imagen.* Salamanca: Ediciones Universidad de Salamanca, 57–70.

Bonazzoli, Francesca, and Michele Robecchi. 2014. *De Mona Lisa a los Simpson.* Barcelona: Planeta.

Boria, Monica *et al.*, eds. 2020. *Translation and Multimodality. Beyond Words.* New York and London: Routledge.

Bourdieu, Pierre. 1979a. *La distinction. Critique social du jugement.* Paris: Minuit.

Bourdieu, Pierre. 1979b. *La fotografía, un arte intermedio.* México: Nueva Imagen.

Bourdieu, Pierre. 1971. "Elementos de una teoría sociológica de la percepción artística", in A. Silberman *et al.*, eds. *Sociología del arte.* Buenos Aires: Nueva Visión.

Bradley, Jessica, and Lou Harvey. 2019. "Creative Inquiry in Applied Linguistics. Language, Communication and the Arts", in Clare Wright, Lou Harvey and James Simpson, eds. *Voices and Practices in Applied Linguistics. Diversifying a Discipline.* New York: White Rose University Press, 91–107.

Brems, Elke, Reine Meylaerts, and Luc van Doorslaer. 2014. "Translation Studies Looking Back and Looking Forward", in Elke Brems, Reine Meylaerts, and Luc van Doorslaer, eds. *The Known Unknowns of Translation Studies.* Amsterdam: John Benjamins, 1–16.

Breytenbach, Breyten. 2009. *Notes from the Middle World.* Chicago, IL: Haymarket Books.

Bronfen, Elisabeth. 2018. *Crossmappings. On Visual Culture.* London: I.B. Tauris.

Broodthaers, Marcel. 1988. "Ten Thousand Francs Reward", in Benjamin H. D. Buchloh, ed. *Broodthaers. Writings, Interviews, Photographs.* Cambridge, MA: The MIT Press.

Bryson, Norman, and Mieke Bal. 1991. "Semiotics and Art History", *Art Bulletin* 73, 2: 174–208.

Bryson, Norman, Michael Ann Holly, and Keith Moxey. 1994. *Visual Culture. Images and Interpretations.* Hannover and London: University Press of New England.

Buddensieg, Andrea, and Peter Weibel, eds. 2007. *Contemporary Art and the Museum. A Global Perspective.* Ostfildern: Hatje Cantz.

Buchloh, Benjamin. 1998/2017. "'Art Is Not About Skill': Benjamin Buchloh Interviews Lawrence Weiner on His Sensual Approach to Conceptual Art", *Artspace* 16 February.

Butler, Emily. 2020. "How Can We Listen Better?" in *Nalini Malani. Can You Hear Me?* London: Whitechapel Gallery, 61–68.

Cage, John. 1979. "_____ (title of composition), _____ (article) _____ (adjective) Circus On _____ (title of book): Means for translating a book into a performance without actors, a performance which is both literary and musical or one or the other." From the pamphlet Book One: John Cage: Roaratorio' (pp. 59–61 [3 of 76]) in the compact disc boxed set *John Cage Vol. 6: Roaratorio; Laughtears; Writing for the Second Time Through Finnegans Wake* (Mode Records 28/29, 1992). Originally published by Henmar Press, 1979, as Edition Peters 66816.

Cage, John. 1961. *Silence*. Middletown, CT: Weyslan University Press.

Çakırlar, Cüneyt. 2013. "Aesthetics of Self-Scaling: Parallaxed Transregionalism and Kutluğ Ataman's Art-Practice", *Critical Arts: South-North Cultural and Media Studies* 27, 6, Special Issue: *Revisiting Ethnographic Turn in Contemporary Art* 2, December: 684–706.

Campbell, Madeleine L. 2017. "Towards a Rhetoric of Translation for the Postdramatic Text", *Poroi* 13, 1: Article 2. https://doi.org/10.13008/2151-2957.1234.

Campbell, Madeleine L., and Laura González. 2018. "'Wozu Image?'/What's the Point of Images? Exploring the Relation between Image and Text through Intersemiotic Translation and Its Embodied Experience", *Open Cultural Studies*, November: 686–699.

Campbell, Madeleine L., and Ricarda Vidal, eds. 2019. *Translating Across Sensory and Linguistic Borders. Intersemiotic Journeys between Media*. New York: Palgrave Macmillan.

Chambers, Iain. 2018. *Location, Borders and Beyond. Thinking with Postcolonial Art*. Worlding the World.

Chambers, Iain. 2017. *Postcolonial Interruptions, Unauthorised Modernities*. London and New York: Rowman & Littlefield.

Chambers, Iain. 2014. "Afterword: After the Museum", in Iain Chambers *et al.*, eds. *The Postcolonial Museum. The Arts of Memory and the Pressures of History*. Surrey: Ashgate, 241–246.

Ch'i Liu, Jui. 2010. "Female Spectatorship and the Masquerade: Cindy Sherman's Untitled Film Stills", *History of Photography* 34, 1: 79–89.

Clarke, Michael. 2007. *Verbalising the Visual. Translating Art and Design into Words*. Lausanne: AVA Publishing.

Clüver, Claus. 2019. "From 'The Mutual Illumination of the Arts' to 'Studies of Intermediality'", *International Journal of Semiotics and Visual Rhetoric* 3: 63–74.

Clüver, Claus. 2007. Intermediality and Interarts Studies", in Jens Arvidson, Mikael Askander, Jørgen Bruhn, and Heidrun Führer, eds. *Changing Borders: Contemporary Positions in Intermediality*. Lund: Intermedia Studies Press, 19–37.

Cohn, Neil. 2018. "In Defense of a 'Grammar' in the Visual Language of Comics", *Journal of Pragmatics* 127, April: 1–19.

Cohn, Neil. 2013. "Visual Narrative Structure", *Cognitive Science* 34: 413–452.

Colby, Georgina. 2012. "Radical Interiors: Cindy Sherman's 'Sex Pictures' and Kathy Acker's *My Mother: Demonology*", *Women. A Cultural Review* 23, 2: 182–200.

Coldiron, A. E. B. 2016. "Introduction: Beyond Babel, or, the Agency of Translators in Early Modern Literature and History", *Philological Quarterly* 95, 3/4: 311–323.

Coleman, Kevin. 2015. "The Right Not to Be Looked At", *Estudios Interdisciplinarios de América Latina y el Caribe* 25, 2: 43–63.

Combalía, Victoria. 2005. *La poética de lo neutro*. Barcelona: Debolsillo.

Connelly, Heather. 2018. "Translation Zone(s): A Stuttering: An Experiential Approach to Linguistic Hospitality", *Open Cultural Studies* 2: 162–174.

Cordingley, Anthony, and Céline Frigau Manning. 2017. "What is Collaborative Translation?" In Anthony Cordingley and Céline Frigau Manning, eds. *Collaborative Translation: From the Renaissance to the Digital Age*. London: Bloomsbury, 1–30.

Crimp, Douglas. 1980. "The Photographic Activity of Postmodernism", *October* 15, Winter: 91–101.

Crimp, Douglas. 1979. "Pictures", *October* 8: 75–88.

Cronin, Michael. 2010. "The Translation Crowd", *Revista Tradumàtica* 8. www.fti. uab.es/tradumatica/revista/num8/articles/04art.htm.

Cronin, Michael. 2003. *Translation and Globalization*. London and New York: Routledge.

Culler, Jonathan. 1983. *On Deconstruction: Theory and Criticism after Structuralism*. Ithaca: Cornell University Press.

Dam, Helle V., Matilde Nisbeth Brogger, and Karen Korning Zethsen, eds. 2019. *Moving Boundaries in Translation Studies*. London: Routledge.

Danto, Arthur. 1991. *History Portraits*. New York: Rizzoli.

Danto, Arthur. 1990. "Photography and Performance: Cindy Sherman's Stills", in Cindy Sherman, ed. *Untitled Film Stills*. New York: Rizzoli, 5–14.

De Diego, Estrella. 2011. *No soy yo. Autobiografía, performance y nuevos espectadores*. Madrid: Siruela.

Delabastita, Dirk. 2003. "Translation Studies for the 21st Century. Trends and Perspectives", *Génesis* 3: 7–24.

Demos, T. J. 2013. *The Migrant Image: The Art and Politics of Documentary during Global Crisis*. Durham, NC and London: Duke University Press.

Derrida, Jacques. 2000. "Hostipitality", trans. Barry Stocker and Forbes Morlock. *Angelaki. Journal of the Theoretical Humanities* 5, 3, December: 3–18.

Derrida, Jacques. 1997/2000. *Of Hospitality*. Trans. Rachel Bowlby. Stanford: Stanford University Press.

Derrida, Jacques. 1982/1985. *The Ear of the Other. Otobiography, Transference, Translation*. Trans. Peggy Kamuf. Lincoln and London: University of Nebraska Press.

Desjardins, Renée. 2017. *Translation and Social Media. In Theory, in Training and in Professional Practice*. London: Palgrave Macmillan.

Desjardins, Renée. 2008. "Inter-Semiotic Translation within the Space of the Multimodal Text", *TranscUlturAl. A Journal of Translation and Cultural Studies* 1. http://ejournals.library.ualberta.ca/index.php/TC/article/view/4144.

D'hulst, Lieven, and Yves Gambier, eds. 2018. *A History of Modern Translation Knowledge*. Amsterdam: John Benjamins.

Di Paola, Modesta. 2018a. "Traducción visual. Epistemología de la traducción en las artes visuales", *Boletín de arte*, núm. 18, septiembre. Universidad Nacional de la Plata.

Di Paola, Modesta. 2018b. "'Re-belle et infidèle'. El feminismo canadiense y sus reflejos en las narrativas artísticas del *in-betweenness*: Mona Hatoum, Chantal Akerman y Ghada Amer", *Anales de Historia del Arte* 28: 133–146.

Di Paola, Modesta. 2017. "La Babel de Cildo Meireles", in *Interartive. A Platform for Contemporary Art and Thought*. https://interartive.org/2015/05/babel-cildo-meireles-di-paola.

Di Paola, Modesta. 2015. *El arte que traduce. 1995–2015. La traducción como mediación cultural en los procesos de transmisión y recepción de las obras de arte*. PhD Dissertation. Universitat de Barcelona.

Diack, Heather. 2020. *Documents of Doubt. The Photographic Conditions of Conceptual Art*. Minneapolis-London: University of Minnesota Press.

Dicerto, Sara. 2018. *Multimodal Pragmatics and Translation: A New Model of Source Text Analysis*. London: Palgrave Macmillan.

Didi-Huberman, Georges. 2018. "Cuando las imágenes tocan lo real", in Georges Didi-Huberman, Clément Chéroux, and Javier Arnaldo, eds. *Cuando las imágenes tocan lo real*. Madrid: Círculo de Bellas Artes, 23–52. Trans. Inés Bértolo.

Didi-Huberman, Georges. 2008. *Cuando las imágenes toman posición. El ojo de la Historia*. Madrid: Antonio Machado Libros.

Didi-Huberman, Georges. 1992. *Ce que nous voyons, ce qui nous regarde*. Paris: Les Éditions de Minuit.

Dollerup, Cay. 2008. "Translation in the Global-Local Tension", in Wang Ning and Sun Yifeng, eds. *Translation, Globalisation and Localisation: A Chinese Perspective*. Clevedon: Multilingual Matters, 31–49.

Dot, Anna. 2019. *Art i Posttraducció. De teories i practiques artístiques digitals*. PhD Dissertation. Universitat de Vic.

Döttinger, Christa. 1995/2012. *Cindy Sherman. History Portraits. The Rebirth of the Painting after the End of Painting*. Verona: Schirmer and Mosel. Trans. Daniel Mufson.

Dovchin, Sender, and Alaistair Pennycook. 2017. "Digital Metroliteracies. Space, Diversity, and Identity", in Kathy A. Mills *et al.*, eds. *Handbook of Writing, Literacies, and Education in Digital Cultures*. London and New York: Routledge, 211–222.

Dovitskaya, Margaret. 2005. *Visual Culture: The Study of Visual Culture after the Cultural Turn*. Cambridge: The MIT Press.

Drucker, Johanna. 1997. *The Dual Muse: The Writer as Artist, the Artist as Writer*. St. Louis: Washington University Gallery of Art.

Dworkin, Craig, and Kenneth Goldsmith. 2011. *Against Expression. An Anthology of Conceptual Writing*. Evanston, IL: Northwestern University Press.

Eco, Umberto. 2003. *Dire quasi la stessa cosa. Esperienze di traduzione*. Milano: Bompiani.

Edmond, Jacob. 2019. *Make It the Same. Poetry in the Age of Global Media*. New York: Columbia University Press.

Elkins, James. 2020. *The End of Diversity in Art Historical Writing*. Berlin: De Gruyter.

Elkins, James. 2012. *Theorizing Visual Studies: Writing Through the Discipline*. London and New York: Routledge.

Elkins, James. 2007. *Is Art History Global?* New York and London: Routledge.

Elkins, James. 2000. *How to Use Your Eyes*. New York and London: Routledge.

Elkins, James *et al.*, eds. 2010. *Art and Globalization*. University Park, PA: The Pennsylvania State University Press.

Elleström, Lars, ed. 2021. *Beyond Media Borders. Intermedial Relations Among Multimodal Media*. 2 vol. New York: Palgrave Macmillan.

Elleström, Lars. 2019. *Transmedial Narration. Narratives and Stories in Different Media*. Saint Philip Street Press.

Elleström, Lars. 2014. *Media Transformation. The Transfer of Media Characteristics among Media*. New York: Palgrave Macmillan.

Elleström, Lars, ed. 2010. *Media Borders, Multimodality and Intermediality*. New York: Palgrave Macmillan.

Ensslin, Astrid. 2010. "Respiratory Narrative: Multimodality and Cybernetic Corporeality in 'Physio-Cybertext'", in Ruth Page, ed. *New Perspectives on Narrative and Multimodality*. London and New York: Routledge, 155–165.

Evans, Robin. 1997. *Translations from Drawing to Building*. Cambridge, MA: The MIT Press.

Evans, Jessica, and Stuart Hall, eds. 1999. *Visual Culture: A Reader*. London: Sage.

Fabbri, Paolo. 2017. *L'efficacia semiotica. Risposte e repliche*. Insegne: Mimesis.

Fabbri, Paolo. 2012. *Elogio di Babele*. Insegne: Mimesis.

Federici, Eleonora, and Marilena Parlati, eds. 2018. *The Body Metaphor. Cultural Images, Literary Perceptions, Linguistic Representations*. Perugia: Morlacchi Editore.

Fillitz, Thomas *et al.*, eds. 2012. *Global Studies: Mapping Contemporary Art and Culture*. Ostfildern: Hatje Cantz.

Finnegan, Ruth. 2015. *Where is language? An Anthropologist's Questions on Language, Literature and Performance*. London: Bloomsbury.

Fischer-Lichte, Erika. 2016. "Introduction: From Comparative Arts to Interart Studies", *Paragrana* 25, 2.

Flynn, Peter, Joep Leerssen, and Luc van Doorslaer. 2016. "On Translated Images, Stereotypes and Disciplines", in Luc van Doorslaer, Peter Flynn and Joep Leerssen, eds. *Interconnecting Translation Studies and Imagology*. Amsterdam and Philadelphia: John Benjamins, 1–18.

Fontcuberta, Joan. 2017. *La cámara de Pandora. La fotografí@ después de la fotografía*. Barcelona: Gustavo Gili.

Fontcuberta, Joan. 2016. *La furia de las imágenes. Notas sobre la post-fotografía*. Barcelona: Galaxia Gutenberg.

Fontcuberta, Joan. 2013. *From Here On. Postphotography in the Age of Internet and the Mobile Phone*. Barcelona: Verlag.

Fontcuberta, Joan, *et al*. 2010. *A través del espejo*. Madrid: La Oficina Ediciones.

Foster, Hal, ed. 1998. *Vision and Visuality*. Seattle: Bay Press.

Foucault, Michel. 1973/1983. *This Is Not a Pipe*. Berkeley: University of California Press. Trans. James Harkness.

Foucault, Michel. 1966. *Les Mots et les Choses*. Paris: Gallimard.

Freedberg, David. 1989. *The Power of Images. Studies in the History and Theory of Response*. Chicago and London: The University of Chicago Press.

Gablik, Suzi. 1976. "The Use of Words", in *Magritte*. London: Thames and Hudson.

Gambier, Yves. 2016. "Rapid and Radical Changes in Translation and Translation Studies", *International Journal of Communication* 10: 887–906.

Gambier, Yves. 2014. "Changing Landscape in Translation", *International Journal of Society, Culture & Language*: 1–12.

Gambier, Yves. 2006. "Multimodality and Audiovisual Translation", in M. Carroll, H. Gerzymisch-Arbogast, and S. Nauert, eds. *MuTra 2006—Audiovisual Translation Scenarios: Conference Proceedings*. Saarland: Advanced Translation Research Centre, 91–98.

Gambier, Yves, and Luc van Doorslaer, eds. 2016. *Border Crossings. Translation Studies and Other Disciplines*. Amsterdam: John Benjamins.

Gambier, Yves, and Luc van Doorslaer, eds. 2009. *The Metalanguage of Translation*. Amsterdam and Philadelphia: John Benjamins.

García, Ofelia, and Li Wei. 2014. *Translanguaging: Language, Bilingualism and Education*. London: Palgrave Macmillan.

García Canclini, Néstor. 2014. *El mundo entero como lugar extraño*. Barcelona: Gedisa.

Gardner, Nathanial. 2010. ". . . Porque era un tema prohibido . . . imágenes en *La noche de Tlatelolco* de Elena Poniatowska", *Amerika* 2: 2–12.

Gardner, Nathanial, and Rosario Martín Ruano. 2015. "Reescritura y paratextualidad en *La noche de Tlatelolco*: la imagen visual en la traducción y la reedición como elemento neutralizador del realismo mágico", *Bulletin of Spanish Studies* XCII.

Garrido, Carlos. 2017. "Imágenes globales y contextos locales. Comparando las bienales de La Habana y Johannesburgo", *Iberoamericana* XVII, 66: 73–87.

Gentzler, Edwin. 2017. *Translation and Rewriting in the Age of Post-Translation Studies*. London and New York: Routledge.

Gentzler, Edwin. 2015. "Translation without Borders", *Translation* 4: 1–15.

Gentzler, Edwin. 2014. "Translation Studies: Pre-Discipline, Discipline, Interdiscipline, and Post-Discipline", *International Journal of Society, Culture & Language*. www.ijscl.net.

Gentzler, Edwin. 2013. "Macro and Micro-Turns in Translation Studies", in Luc van Doorslaer and Peter Flynn, eds. *Eurocentrism in Translation Studies*. Amsterdam: John Benjamins, 9–28.

Gentzler, Edwin. 2008. *Translation and Identity in the Americas. New Directions in Translation Theory*. London and New York: Routledge.

Gentzler, Edwin. 2003. "Interdisciplinary Connections", *Perspectives* 11, 1: 11–24.

Giannakopoulou, Vasso. 2019. "Introduction: Intersemiotic Translation as Adaptation", *Adaptation* 12, 3: 199–205.

Goldsmith, Kenneth. 2015. *Theory*. Paris: Jean Boîte Éditions.

Goldsmith, Kenneth. 2011. *Uncreative Writing*. New York: Columbia University Press.

Gorlée, Dinda L. 1997. "Hacia una semiótica textual peirciana", *Signa: revista de la Asociación Española de Semiótica* 6: 308–326.

Grijelmo, Alex. 2000. *La seducción de las palabras*. Madrid: Santillana.

Grønstad, Asbjørn, and Øyvind Vågnes. 2017. "Images and their Incarnations: An Interview with W.J.T. Mitchell", in Kresimis Purgar, ed. *W.J.T. Mitchell's Image Theory. Living Pictures*. New York and London: Routledge, 182–194.

Guasch, Anna María. 2018. *The Codes of the Global in the Twenty-first Century*. Barcelona: Universitat de Barcelona. Trans. Paul E. Davies.

Guasch, Anna María. 2016. *El arte en la era de lo global. 1989/2015*. Madrid: Alianza.

Hall, Stuart, ed. 1997/2003. *Representation. Cultural Representations and Signifying Practices*. London: Sage.

Han, Byung-Chul. 2013/2017. *In the Swarm*. London: The MIT Press. Trans. Erik Butler.

Han, Byung-Chul. 2011/2017. *Shanzhai. El arte de la falsificación y la deconstrucción en China*. Buenos Aires: Caja Negra. Trans. Paula Kuffer.

Haraway, Donna. 1991. *Simians, Cyborgs, and Women: The Reinvention of Nature*. London: Free Association Books.

Harvey, David. 2006. *Spaces of Global Capitalism. Towards a Theory of Uneven Geographical Development*. London and New York: Routledge.

Hayles, N. Katherine, and Jessica Pressman, eds. 2013. *Comparative Textual Media: Transforming the Humanities in the Postprint Era*. Minneapolis: University of Minnesota Press.

Heywood, Ian, and Barry Sandywell. 2011. *The Handbook of Visual Culture*. Oxford: Berg.

Hermans, Theo. 2002. "Paradoxes and Aporia in Translation and Translation Studies", in Alessandra Riccardi, ed. *Translation Studies: Perspectives on an Emerging Discipline*. Cambridge: Cambridge University Press.

Hermans, Theo. 2001. "La traducción y la relevancia de la auto-referencia", in Román Álvarez, ed. *Cartografías de la traducción. Del post-estructuralismo al multiculturalismo*. Salamanca: Ediciones Colegio de España. Trans. M. Rosario Martín Ruano and Jesús Torres.

Hockney, David, and Martin Gayford. 2016. *Una historia de las imágenes. De la caverna a la pantalla del ordenador*. Madrid: Siruela. Trans. Julio Hermoso.

Hofstadter, Douglas R. 2007. *I Am a Strange Loop*. New York: Basic Books.

Hofstadter, Douglas R. 1997. *Le Ton Beau de Marot: In Praise of the Music of Language*. London: Bloomsbury.

Hofstadter, Douglas R. 1979/2013. *Gödel, Escher, Bach*. Barcelona: Tusquets. Trans. Mario Arnaldo Usabiaga and Alejandro López.

Hollander, John. 1995. *The Gazer's Spirit: Poems Speaking to Silent Works of Art*. Chicago: University of Chicago Press.

Holtaway, Jessica. 2021. *World-Forming and Contemporary Art*. London and New York: Routledge.

Hudstvedt, Siri. 2012/2013. *Vivir, pensar, mirar*. Barcelona: Anagrama. Trans. Cecilia Ceriani.

Huntington, Samuel P. 1996. *The Clash of Civilizations and the Remaking of World Order*. New York: Simon & Schuster.

Ianniciello, Celeste. 2018. *Migration, Art and Postcoloniality in the Mediterranean*. London: Routledge.

Jaworski, Adam. 2014. "Metrolingual Art: Multilingualism and Heteroglossia", *International Journal of Bilingualism* 18, 2: 134–158.

Jaworski, Adam, and Crispin Thurlow. 2010. *Semiotic Landscapes. Language, Image, Space*. London and New York: Continuum.

Jay, Martin. 1993. *Downcast Eyes: The Denigration of Vision in Twentieth-Century French Thought*. Berkeley: California University Press.

Jencks, Charles, ed. 1995. *Visual Culture*. London and New York: Routledge.

Jewitt, Carey. 2009. "An Introduction to Multimodality", in Carey Jewitt, ed. *The Routledge Handbook of Multimodal Analysis*. London and New York: Routledge, 14–27.

Jewitt, Carey, Jeff Bezemer, and Kay O'Halloran. 2016. *Introducing Multimodality*. London and New York: Routledge.

Jiménez Crespo, Miguel Ángel. 2017. *Crowdsourcing and Online Collaborative Translations*. Amsterdam: John Benjamins.

Jiménez Hurtado, Catalina, Tiina Tuominen, and Anne Ketola, eds. 2018. "Methods for the Study of Multimodality in Translation", *Linguistica Antverpiensia* 17, online journal.

Johnston, David. 2017. "Prólogo", in Mª Carmen África Vidal Claramonte, ed. *Dile que le he escrito un* blues. *Del texto como partitura a la partitura como traducción en la literatura latinoamericana*. Madrid and Frankfurt: Vervuert Iberoamericana, 11–14.

Johnston, David. 2013. "Professing Translation. The Acts-in-Between", *Target* 25, 3: 365–384.

Jones, Amelia. 1997. "Tracing the Subject with Cindy Sherman", in Amada Cruz *et al.*, eds. *Cindy Sherman: Retrospective*. London: Thames & Hudson, 33–42.

Joyce, James. 1922/1992. *Ulysses*. New York: Penguin.

Kaindl, Klaus. 2020. "A Theoretical Framework for a Multimodal Conception of Translation", in Monica Boria *et al.*, eds. *Translation and Multimodality. Beyond Words*. New York and London: Routledge, 49–70.

Kaindl, Klaus. 2013. "Multimodality and Translation", in Carmen Millán and Francesca Bartrina, eds. *The Routledge Handbook of Translation Studies*. New York and London: Routledge, 257–269.

Kalyva, Eve. 2016. *Image and Text in Conceptual Art. Critical Operations on Context*. New York: Palgrave-Macmillan.

Katan, David. 2016. "Translation at the Cross-Roads: Time for the Transcreational Turn?" *Perspectives* 24, 3: 365–381.

Kim, Yu Yeon. 2001. *Translated Acts. Performance and Body Art from East Asia. 1990–2001*. Berlin: The Haus der Kulturen der Welt.

Kim-Cohen, Seth. 2013. *Against Ambience and Other Essays*. New York: Bloomsbury Academic.

Kinna, Ruth, and Gillian Whiteley, eds. 2020. *Cultures of Violence. Visual Arts and Political Violence*. London and New York: Routledge.

Krauss, Rosalind. 1986. *The Originality of the Avant-Garde and Other Modernist Myths*. Cambridge, MA: The MIT Press.

Kress, Gunther. 2010. *Multimodality. A Social Semiotic Approach to Communication*. London: Routledge.

Kress, Gunther. 2003. *Literacy in the New Media Age*. London: Routledge.

Kress, Gunther, and Theo van Leeuwen. 2001. *Multimodal Discourse. The Modes and Media of Contemporary Communication*. London: Hodder Arnold.

Kress, Gunther, and Theo van Leeuwen. 1996. *Reading Images. The Grammar of Visual Design*. London: Routledge.

Krieger, Murray. 1991. *Ekphrasis. The Illusion of Natural Sign*. Baltimore and London: The Johns Hopkins University Press.

Kristeva, Julia. 1974. *La revolution du langage poétique*. Paris: Éditions du Seuil.

Kosuth, Joseph. 1991. *Art After Philosophy and After: Collective Writings, 1966–1990*. Cambridge, MA: MIT Press. Ed. Gabrielle Guercio.

Lee, Tong King, ed. 2021a. *The Routledge Handbook of Translation and the City*. London and New York: Routledge.

Lee, Tong King. 2021b. "Distribution and Translation", *Applied Linguistics Review* (Ahead of Print). https://doi.org/10.1515/applirev-2020-0139.

Lee, Tong King. 2015a. *Experimental Chinese Poetry. Translation, Technology, Poetics*. Leiden and Boston: Brill.

Lee, Tong King. 2015b. "Translanguaging and Visuality: Translingual Practices in Literary Art", *Applied Linguistics Review* 6, 4: 441–465.

Lee, Tong King. 2014a. "Visuality and Translation in Contemporary Chinese Literary Art: Xu Bing's *A Book from the Sky* and *A Book from the Ground*", *Asia Pacific Translation and Intercultural Studies* 1, 1: 43–62.

Lee, Tong King. 2014b. "Translation, Materiality, Intersemioticity: Excursions in Experimental literature", *Semiotica* 202: 345–364.

Lee, Tong King. 2013a. *Translating the Multilingual City*. Oxford: Peter Lang.

Lee, Tong King. 2013b. "Performing Multimodality: Literary Translation, Intersemioticity and Technology", *Perspectives* 21, 2: 241–256.

Lee, Tong King. 2011. "Translation (De)construction in Contemporary Chinese Poetics. A Case Study of Hsia Yü's Pink Noise", *The Translator* 17, 1: 1–24.

Lee, Tong King, and Li Wei. 2020. "Translanguaging and Momentarity in Social Interaction", in Anna de Fina and Alexandra Georgakopolou, eds. *The Cambridge Handbook of Discourse* Studies. Cambridge: Cambridge University Press, 394–416.

Lingis, Alphonso. 1994. *The Community of Those Who Have Nothing in Common*. Bloomington and Indianapolis: Indiana University Press.

Littau, Karen. 2016. "Translation and the Materialities of Communication", *Translation Studies* 9, 1: 82–96.

Lucie-Smith, Edward. 1984. *Movements in Art since 1945*. New York: Thames and Hudson.

Lyotard, François. 1987. *Que peindre? Adami Arawaka Buren*. Paris: Éditions de la Difference.

Maiorani, Arianna. 2021. *Kinesemiotics: Modelling How Choreographed Movement Means in Space*. New York and London: Routledge.

Maitland, Sarah. 2017. *What is Cultural Translation?* London: Bloomsbury.

Malmkjær, Kirsten. 2019. *Translation and Creativity*. New York and London: Routledge.

Marais, Kobus. 2019. *A (Bio)Semiotic Theory of Translation: The Emergence of Social-Cultural Reality*. London and New York: Routledge.

Marais, Kobus, and Reine Meylaerts, eds. 2019. *Complexity Thinking in Translation Studies. Methodological Considerations*. London and New York: Routledge.

Marciniak, Katarzyna, and Imogen Tyler, eds. 2014. *Immigrant Protest: Politics, Aesthetics and Everyday Dissent*. Albany: State University of New York.

Martín Ruano, M. Rosario. 2018. "Legal and Institutional Translation", in Roberto Valdeón and M.C. África Vidal, eds. *The Routledge Handbook of Spanish Translation Studies*. London and New York: Routledge.

Martínez Luna, Sergio. 2012. "La visualidad en cuestión y el derecho a mirar", *Revista Chilena de Antropología Visual* 19: 20–36.

Massidda, Serenella. 2015. *Audiovisual Translation in the Digital Age: The Italian Fansubbing Phenomenon*. London: Palgrave Macmillan.

Mateo, Marta. 2012. "Music and Translation", in Yves Gambier and Luc van Doorslaer, eds. *Handbook of Translation Studies*, vol. 3. Amsterdam and Philadelphia: John Benjamins, 115–121.

Matt, Gerald. 2000. "In Conversation with Shirin Neshat", in *Shirin Neshat*. Wien: Kunsthalle.

Mazzara, Federica. 2019. *Reframing Migration: Lampedusa, Border Spectacle and the Aesthetics of Subversion*. Frankfurt: Peter Lang.

McClary, Susan. 1991/2002. *Feminine Endings: Music, Gender & Sexuality*. Minnesota: University of Minnesota Press.

McMurtrie, Robert James. 2017. *The Semiotics of Movement in Space*. New York and London: Routledge.

Mersmann, Birgit, and Alexandra Schneider, eds. 2009. *Transmission Image: Visual Translation and Cultural Agency*. Newcastle: Cambridge Scholars Publishing.

Minissale, Gregory. 2013. *The Psychology of Contemporary Art*. Cambridge: Cambridge University Press.

Minissale, Gregory. 2009. *Framing Consciousness in Art. Transcultural Perspectives*. Amsterdam and New York: Rodopi.

Minors, Helen Julia. 2020. "Translations Between Music and Dance: Analysing the Choreomusical Gestural Interplay in Twentieth- and Twenty-First Century Dance Works", in Monica Boria *et al.*, eds. *Translation and Multimodality. Beyond Words*. New York and London: Routledge, 158–178.

Minors, Helen Julia. 2014. *Music, Text and Translation*. London: Continuum.

Mirzoeff, Nicholas. 2016. *How to See the World*. New York: Basic Books.

Mirzoeff, Nicholas. 2011a. *The Right to Look. A Counterhistory of Visuality*. Durham: Duke University Press.

Mirzoeff, Nicholas. 2011b. "The Right to Look", *Critical Inquiry* 37, 3, Spring: 473–496.

Mirzoeff, Nicholas. 2006. "On Visuality", *Journal of Visual Culture* 5, 1: 53–79.

Mirzoeff, Nicholas. 1999. *An Introduction to Visual Culture*. London: Routledge.

Mirzoeff, Nicholas. 1998. *The Visual Culture Reader*. New York and London: Routledge.

Mirzoeff, Nicholas. 1995. *Bodyscape. Art, Modernity and the Ideal Figure*. London and New York: Routledge.

Mitchell, William John T. 2005. *What Do Pictures Want? The Lives and Loves of Images*. Chicago and London: The University of Chicago Press.

Mitchell, William John T. 2003. *Me++the Cyborg Self and the Networked City*. Cambridge, MA: The MIT Press.

Mitchell, William John T. 2002. "Showing Seeing: A Critique of Visual Culture", *Journal of Visual Culture* 1, 2: 165–181.

Mitchell, William John T. 1994. *Picture Theory*. Chicago: The University of Chicago Press.

Mitchell, William John T. 1986. *Iconology. Image, Text, Ideology*. Chicago: The University of Chicago Press.

Morin, Edgar. 1990/2008. *On Complexity*. Cresskill: Hampton Press. Trans. Robin Postel.

Morra, Joanne. 2000. "Translation into Art History", *Parallax* 6, 1: 129–138.

Morris, Catherine. 1999. *The Essential Cindy Sherman*. New York: The Wonderland Press.

Moxey, Keith. 2008. "Visual Studies and the Iconic Turn", *Journal of Visual Culture* 7, 2, August: 131–146.

Mulvey, Laura. 1989/2009. *Visual and Other Pleasures*. New York: Palgrave Macmillan.

Mulvey, Laura. 1991. "A Phantasmagoria of the Female Body: The Work of Cindy Sherman", *New Left Review* 188, July/August: 136–150.

Mulvey, Laura. 1975. "Visual Pleasure and Narrative Cinema", *Screen* 16, 3: 6–18.

Muntadas, Antoni. 2008. "On Translation. Project Notes", in *Muntadas. La construcción del miedo y la pérdida de lo público*. Granada: Centro José Guerrero.

Neumark, Norie, Ross Gibson, and Theo van Leeuwen, eds. 2010. *Voice: Vocal Aesthetics in Digital Arts and Media*. Cambridge, MA: The MIT Press.

Oittinen, Riitta, Anne Ketola, and Melissa Garavini. 2019. *Translating Picturebooks. Revoicing the Verbal, the Visual and the Aural for a Child Audience*. New York and London: Routledge.

Olteanu, Alin *et al.*, eds. 2019. *Meanings & Co. The Interdisciplinarity of Communication, Semiotics and Multimodality*. New York: Springer.

O'Sullivan, Carol, and Caterina Jeffcote, eds. 2013. "Special Issue on Translating Multimodalities", *Journal of Specialized Translation* 20, July, online journal.

Ott, Michaela, and Thomas Weber, eds. 2019. *Situated in Translations: Cultural Communities and Media Practices*. Bielefeld: Transcript Verlag.

Owens, Craig. 1992. *Beyond Recognition. Representation, Power, and Culture*. Berkeley: University of California Press.

Page, Ruth, ed. 2010. *New Perspectives on Narrative and Multimodality*. London and New York: Routledge.

Page, Ruth, and Bronwen Thomas, eds. 2011. *New Narratives. Stories and Storytelling in the Digital Age*. Lincoln and London: University of Nebraska Press.

Papastergiadis, Nikos. 2012. *Cosmopolitanism and Culture*. Cambridge. Polity Press.

Pârlog, Aba-Carina. 2019. *Intersemiotic Translation. Literary and Linguistic Multimodality*. New York: Palgrave Macmillan.

Peck, Amiena, and Christopher Stroud. 2015. "Skinscapes", *Linguistic Landscape* 1, 1/2: 133–151.

Pennycook, Alastair. 2018. *Posthumanist Applied Linguistics*. New York and London: Routledge.

Pennycook, Alastair. 2017. "Translanguaging and Semiotic Assemblages", *International Journal of Multilingualism* 14, 3: 269–282.

Pennycook, Alastair, and Emi Otsuji. 2015. *Metrolingualism: Language and the City*. London: Routledge.

Pérez-González, Luis. 2014. "Multimodality in Translation and Interpreting Studies", in Sandra Bermann and Catherine Porter, eds. *A Companion to Translation Studies*. Chichester: Wiley-Blackwell, 119–131.

Perloff, Marjorie. 2010. *Unoriginal Genius: Poetry by Other Means in the New Century*. Chicago: The University of Chicago Press.

Perloff, Marjorie. 2004. "The Oulipo Factor: The Procedural Poetics of Caroline Bergvall and Christian Bok", *Textual Practice* 18, 1: 23–45.

Pink, Sarah. 2007. *Doing Visual Ethnography: Images, Media and Representation in Research*. London: Sage.

Pink, Sarah. 2006. *The Future of Visual Anthropology: Engaging the Senses*. London: Routledge.

Pinney, Christopher. 2011. *Photography and Anthropology*. London: Reaktion Books.

Pultz Moslund, Sten *et al.*, eds. 2015. *The Culture of Migration: Politics, Aesthetics and Histories*. London and New York: Tauries.

Rabourdin, Caroline. 2020. *Sense in Translation: Essays on the Bilingual Body*. London and New York: Routledge.

Rabourdin, Caroline. 2016a. "Spatial Translations and Embodied Bilingualism: Defining the Migrant's Experience from an Architectural Perspective", *CALL: Irish Journal for Culture, Arts, Literature and Language* 1, 1: 1–15.

Rabourdin, Caroline. 2016b. "Walking and Writing: Paul Auster's Map of the Tower of Babel", in Emmanuelle Peraldo, ed. *Literature and Geography. The Writing of Space through History*. Cambridge: Cambridge Scholars Publishing, 222–233.

Ramos Pinto, Sara, and Elisabetta Adami. 2020. "Traduire dans un monde de signes non traduits: l'incidence de la multimodalité en traductologie", *Meta* 65, 1: 9–28.

Ravelli, Louise J., and Robert James McMurtrie. 2016. *Multimodality in the Built Environment: Spatial Discourse Analysis*. New York and London: Routledge.

Raw, Laurence. 2012. *Translation, Adaptation and Transformation*. London: Bloomsbury.

Ring Petersen, Anne. 2017. *Migration into Art: Transcultural Identities and Art-making in a Globalized World*. Manchester: Manchester University Press.

Rizzo, Alexandra. 2019. "Translating Migration in the Visual Arts: *Calais Children* and *Project #RefugeeCameras* as Collaborative Aesthetic Counter Narratives", in Eleonora Federici, Rosario Martín and África Vidal, eds. *I-LanD Journal—Special Issue: Translating and Interpreting Linguistic and Cultural Differences in a Migrant Era*, April. Napoli: Paolo Loffredo Editore.

Robillard, Valerie, and Els Jongeneel, eds. 1998. *Pictures into Words. Theoretical and Descriptive Approaches to Ekphrasis*. Amsterdam: VU University Press.

Rorty, Richard M. ed. 1967. *The Linguistic Turn. Essay in Philosophical Method*. Chicago: The University of Chicago Press.

Rose, Gillian. 2001/2007. *Visual Methodologies: An Introduction to the Interpretation of Visual Materials*. London: Sage.

Rose, Gillian, and Divya P. Tolia-Kelly, eds. 2012. *Visuality/Materiality. Images, Objects and Practices*. Surrey: Ashgate.

Said, Edward. 1993. *Culture and Imperialism*. New York: Alfred Knopf.

Saletnik, Jeffrey. 2012. "John Cage and the Task of the Translator", *Art in Translation* 4, 1, March: 73–88.

Salmose, Niklas, and Lars Elleström, eds. 2020. *Transmediations: Communication Across Media Borders*. New York and London: Routledge.

Saloni, Mathur, ed. 2011. *The Migrant's Time, Rethinking Art History and Diaspora*. Williamstown, MA: The Sterling and Francine Clark Art Institute.

Schimanski, Johan, and Stephen F. Wolfe, eds. 2017. *Border Aesthetics: Concepts and Intersections*. New York: Berghahn.

Schramm, Moritz, *et al*. 2019. *Reframing Migration, Diversity and the Arts: The Postmigrant Condition*. London and New York: Routledge.

Schwenger, Peter. 2019. *Asemic. The Art of Writing*. Minneapolis: Minnesota University Press.

Sennett. Richard. 2003. *El respeto. Sobre la dignidad del hombre en un mundo de desigualdad*. Barcelona: Anagrama. Trans. Marco Aurelio Galmarini.

Serafini, Paula. 2018. *Performance Action. The Politics of Art Activism*. London and New York: Routledge.

Serres, Michel. 1983. "Noise", *SubStance* 12, 3, 40: 48–60.

Serres, Michel. 1982. *Hermes: Literature, Science, Philosophy*. Baltimore, MD: Johns Hopkins University Press. Ed. J. V. Harari and D. F. Bell.

Shapiro, Michael J. 2013. *Studies in Trans-Disciplinary Method: After the Aesthetic Turn*. London and New York: Routledge.

Sheren, Ila Nicole. 2015. *Portable Borders: Performance Art and Politics on the U.S. Frontera since 1984*. Austin. University of Texas Press.

Silverman, Kaja. 1996. *The Threshold of the Visible World*. New York and London: Routledge.

Simon, Sherry. 2019. *Translation Sites*. London and New York: Routledge.

Simon, Sherry. 2012. *Cities in Translation. Intersections of Language and Memory*. London and New York: Routledge.

Smith, Marquard. 2008. *Visual Culture Studies: Interviews with Key Thinkers*. London: Sage.

Smith, Marquard. 2005. "Visual Studies, or the Ossification of Thought", *Journal of Visual Culture* 4, 237.

Smith, Terry. 2017. *One and Five Ideas. On Conceptual Art and Conceptualism*. Durham and London: Duke University Press.

Smith, Terry. 2013. "Contemporary Art: World Currents in Transition Beyond Globalization", in Hans Belting *et al*., eds. *The Global Contemporary: The Rise of New Art World after 1989*. Cambridge, MA: MIT Press for ZKM, Karlsruhe.

Smith, Terry. 1990. "The Tasks of Translation: Art & Language in Australia & New Zealand 1975–6", in Ian Wedde and Gregory Burke, eds. *Now See Hear! Art, Language and Translation*. Wellington, New Zealand: Victoria University Press, 253–254.

Solomon-Godeau, Abigail. 1991a. "Sexual Difference: Both Sides of the Camera", in *Photography at the Dock: Essays on Photographic History, Institutions, and Practices*. Minneapolis: University of Minnesota, 272–274.

Solomon-Godeau, Abigail. 1991b. "Suitable for Framing: The Critical Recasting of Cindy Sherman", *Parkett* 29: 112–115.

Sontag, Susan. 1966. *Styles of Radical Will*. New York: Picador.

Spinzi, Cinzia, Alessandra Rizzo, and Marianna Lya Zummo, eds. 2018. *Translation or Transcreation? Discourses, Texts, and Visuals*. New Castle upon Tyne: Cambridge Scholars Publishing.

Steyn, Juliet, and Nadja Stamselberg, eds. 2014. *Breaching Borders: Art, Migration and the Metaphor of Waste*. London: Tauris & Co.

Steinberg, Leo. 1981. "Velasquez' *Las Meninas*", *October* 19: 45–54.

Steiner, George. 1976. *Language and Silence*. New York: Atheneum.

Sturge, Kate. 2007. *Representing Others. Translation, Ethnography and the Museum*. Manchester: St. Jerome.

Sturken, Marita, and Lisa Cartwright. 2009. *Practices of Looking: An Introduction to Visual Culture*. Oxford and New York: Oxford University Press.

Susam-Sarajeva, Sebnem. 2018. "Music, Politics and Translation", in Fruela Fernández and Jonathan Evans, eds. *The Routledge Handbook of Translation and Politics*. London and New York: Routledge, 358–367.

Susam-Sarajeva, Sebnem. 2008. "Translation and Music. Changing Perspectives, Frameworks and Significance", *The Translator. Translation and Music* 14, 2: 187–200.

Tello, Verónica. 2016. *Counter-Memorial Aesthetics. Refugee Histories and the Politics of Contemporary Art*. London: Bloomsbury.

Torop, Peeter. 1995. *Totalny perevod*. Tartu: Tartu University Press.

Trojanow, Ilija, and Ranjit Hoskoté. 2007. *Kampfabsage: Kulturen behämpfen sich nicht -sie flieben zusammen*. Munich: Blessing.

Tymoczko, Maria. 2007. *Enlarging Translation, Empowering Translators*. Manchester: St. Jerome.

van Doorslaer, Luc, and Peter Flynn, eds. 2013. *Eurocentrism in Translation Studies*. Amsterdam: John Benjamins.

van Leeuwen, Theo. 2021. *Multimodality and Identity*. London and New York: Routledge.

van Leeuwen, Theo. 2010. *The Language of Colour: An Introduction*. London and New York: Routledge.

Venuti, Lawrence. 2010. "Ekphrasis, Translation, Critique", *Art in Translation* 2, 2: 131–152.

Vidal Claramonte, MªCarmen África. In press. "Translating Fear in Border Spaces: Antoni Muntadas' *On Translation: Fear/Miedo/Jauf*", *Cráter*.

Vidal Claramonte, MªCarmen África. 2020. "Fluid Borders: From *Carmen* to *the Car Man*", in Adriana Şerban and Kelly Kar Yue Chan, eds. *Opera and Translation. Unity and Diversity*. Amsterdam: John Benjamins, 95–115.

Vidal Claramonte, MªCarmen África. 2019. "Violins, Violence, Translation: Looking Outwards", *The Translator* 25, 3, eds. David Johnston and Susan Bassnett.

Vidal Claramonte, MªCarmen África. 2017. *"Dile que le he escrito un blues". Del texto como partitura a la partitura como traducción en la literatura latinoamericana*. Madrid and Frankfurt: Vervuert Iberoamericana.

Vidal Claramonte, MªCarmen África. 2016. "On the Noises and Rhythms of Translation", *Translation and Interpreting Studies* 11, 2, July: 131–151.

Vidal Claramonte, MªCarmen África. 2012. *La traducción y los espacios: viajes, mapas, fronteras*. Granada: Comares.

Voegelin, Salomé. 2018. *The Political Possibility of Sound. Fragments of Listening*. New York and London: Bloomsbury.

Weibel, Peter. 2017. "The Global Contemporary and the Rise of New Art Worlds. Globalization and Contemporary Art", *Transnazionale* 1, 1, March: 9–22.

Weissbrod, Rachel, and Ayelet Kohn. 2019. *Translating the Visual. A Multimodal Perspective*. London and New York: Routledge.

Weiner, Lawrence. 1972. "In Conversation with Ursula Meyer" (*October* 12, 1969), in Ursula Meyer, ed. *Conceptual Art*. New York: Dutton.

Welish, Marjorie. 1996. "Lawrence Weiner", *Bomb* 54, Winter: 10–15.

Welish, Marjorie, Robert Barry, Martha Rosler, and Nancy Spero. 1994. "Word into Image: Robert Barry, Martha Rosler and Nancy Spero", *Bomb* 47, Spring: 36–44.

Williamson, Sophie J., ed. 2019. *Translation*. Cambridge, MA: The MIT Press.

Wilson, Rita, and Brigid Maher, eds. 2012. *Words, Images and Performances in Translation*. London and New York: Continuum.

Wolf, Michaela, and Alexandra Fukari. 2007. *Constructing a Sociology of Translation*. Amsterdam: John Benjamins.

Zwischenberger, Cornelia. 2019. "From Inward to Outward: The Need for Translation Studies to Become Outward-Going", *The Translator. The "Outward Turn"* 25, 3: 256–268.

Zwischenberger, Cornelia. 2017. "Translation as a Metaphoric Traveler across Disciplines. Wanted: Translaboration!" In Alexa Alfer, ed. *'Translaboration' Translation as Collaboration*, special issue of *Translation and Translanguaging in Multilingual Contexts* 3, 3: 388–406.

Index

For Product Safety Concerns and Information please contact our EU
representative GPSR@taylorandfrancis.com Taylor & Francis Verlag GmbH,
Kaufingerstraße 24, 80331 München, Germany

Printed and bound by CPI Group (UK) Ltd, Croydon, CR0 4YY

11/04/2025

01844010-0007